Abiding Love

Reflections From The Heart by Widows and Widowers

Compiled by Shenita Connally

Published by Still Standing Publishing Company
Book Cover Design: Creative Scales Design
Creative Direction: Shenita Connally

Printed in the United States of America

ISBN- 9781791701628

IN LOVING MEMORY OF

Burrell Carroll Billingslea II

David Dwayne Bishop, Sr.

Aquilla Jones Causey

Jerome Clay, Jr.

Winston Connally

Jake Davis, Jr.

Jamal Hisheam Hodge

Lisa Poller Horton

Brian Ja'mez Logan

Rudolph Long

Chad Edward Rivas, Sr.

John Francis Sewell, Jr.

Sherri Shaw

Calvin Spoon

Gary Rogers Warren, Sr.

Rodney Anquoine Webb

Anthony Weems

ACKNOWLEDGEMENT

Thank you, God, who is the head of our lives.

Thank you to our families, friends, and supporters.

Thank you to this amazing team of authors for being transparent and for sharing your stories of Abiding Love.

INTRODUCTION

Dear Reader,

Thank you for sharing in this journey of Abiding Love with us! It is our heart's desire that this book will bless you immensely. As you read through the stories, you will be inspired, informed, and entertained. You may even laugh or cry.

God gave me this vision to share the love I experienced with my husband and still do today, but I couldn't share it alone. As a result of launching Life After the Rain, an event that is specifically for widows and widowers, I developed a family of likeminded individuals who also shared this Abiding Love for their spouses. These stories share the thoughts, emotions and situations experienced by each author. The dialogue and feelings are raw and uncensored.

Some of us are still widows and widowers, while others have opened their hearts to experience love again. Sit back, relax, and enjoy the journeys of Abiding Love.

Shenita Connally

FOREWORD

Today we live in a society of people who have not experienced the true depths of love, and as a result, many have a surface knowledge of what true love entails. The Apostle Paul gives us a picture of true love in Romans 5:8 which says, "But God showed His great love for us by sending Christ to die for us while we were still sinners." It is ironic to me that while God exhibits great love for us even in the bleakest of circumstances/times, it is during these tough times that many people walk away – yet they declare with their mouths they have great "love" for us.

There is no doubt that our society and our experiences tend to shape our thinking. What we see, hear, and feel all play a role in molding us into the persons we ultimately become. Many years ago, famed duo, Ike and Tina Turner, made famous a song entitled, "What's Love Got To Do With It." Like the words of the song, many believe that love is nothing more than "a second-hand emotion", but I submit to you, many of those individuals have never experienced true love.

True love is an abiding love. True love sees into one and supplies unspoken needs. True love "abides" well after the one loved leaves. This book is a compilation of thoughts and stories of individuals who have experienced true abiding love.

I must admit that I did not fully understand the implications of abiding love until I sat with two widows who truly loved and were loved by their husbands. As I spoke with them and listened to their stories, I was struck with the fact that they had truly experienced love on a level that few ever do. I was able to see why their hearts continued to flow with an undying, unyielding love towards the spouse they had "lost" – only to recognize they had not "lost" them at all. Because of the great love they had shared together, that love remained, even though their spouses were physically gone. Hence, the subject of this book – Abiding Love.

I invite you to take a fascinating journey into the lives of several individuals who have experienced "Abiding Love" and glean the truths, triumphs, and tests of love. Abiding Love will help you understand that nothing can truly separate you from the love you experience. Love remains well after those you love leave.

"And now these three remain (abide): faith, hope, and love. But the greatest of these is love. (1 Cor 13:13).

In His Grace,

Marquis D. Jones, Author

IN HONOR OF
ELDER CHAD RIVAS, SR. AND
MINISTER WINSTON CONNALLY

A few days ago, an open invitation was extended to friends and family, to attend a dinner hosted in honor of a deceased friend by his wife. The purpose was to reminisce and celebrate the life of our friend/her husband. I originally accepted the invitation, but as the time drew near, I began to have second thoughts about whether or not I wanted to attend. In my mind, I did not want to sit around and grieve the loss again, as it is my custom to try and remember those who transition as they were in life, rather than in death. Nevertheless, I made my way over to the home. When I arrived, there were a number of guests already inside and they were deep into conversation. I spoke, put my items down, and went in to partake of the conversation. To my surprise, it was not macabre, but rather joyous. It was a time of sharing and reflecting as to how our friend impacted each of our lives and the imprint he left on our hearts and minds. One of the guests there had also lost her husband, just a month prior. I knew both men and interacted with them in my local church, as they were leaders in our assembly. I knew them both to be upstanding gentlemen, and statesmen in their own right.

As I listened to the widows speak about their husbands, I began to recognize that love abides. The second lady said, "People think that because someone dies, the love stops. It does not. Even though the life has ended, love remains." It was not until that moment that I recognized the **truth** in what she spoke ...And then I saw why God chose to be love. Out of all the fruit of the Spirit, of all the things God Himself could be – He chose to be love. Why? **Because love abides**. To abide is to live on, even after that which is physical goes away, love abides. To abide is to live within. Love is more than a feeling, yet it rises up on the inside of us and fills the atmosphere when it is shared. These two women, having been truly loved by their husbands, had experienced something that many people never get to experience – true love. And yet, they are two very different women, who share the similar experience of losing their mates - their paths, crossed by a common thread – true love. I sat there in awe of the strength, courage and tenacity of them both. Although both husbands are gone – love abides.

It was amazing to see their hearts leap, their countenance brighten, as they spoke of their husbands. It was evident that God had visited them both, not only while their husbands were here physically, but also after they had transitioned. This abiding love was/is still evident in their lives. They both had a glow about them as they reminisced about the love of their lives. My pre-conceived notions were obliterated as I began to take in the wisdom of God shared from two different perspectives. I then understood that God wanted me there to show me a picture of true love. Love is not a second-hand emotion. Love is life, love is God, and love is abiding.

Thank you, ladies - my friends - for allowing God to teach others through you.

Multiplied Grace,

Marquis D. Jones
07/11/16

TABLE OF CONTENTS

AN AGELESS LOVE AFFAIR
Janice Gregg Billingslea

The most joyous occasion is the union of Man and Woman in the Celebration of Life

Burrell, Love of my life, I have the pleasure and honor of co-authoring a book entitled, "Abiding Love," an anthology of love letters from widows and widowers written to our spouses posthumously. For me, this is a daunting endeavor. Moreover, I am limited to using just 1000 words to express the overwhelming plethora of emotions and experiences that have arisen out of this tragic experience. Too few to adequately describe my life without you and my tremendously wonderful, sometimes tumultuous, life with you as your student, friend, wife, lover, and mother of our children. Burrell, living without you is inarguably the hardest task that I have ever attempted in my life. However, I am honored to share my memoirs with the world describing the simply wonderful complex man that you were. So, I will attempt to complete this letter to you that I began almost four years ago.

Dearest Burrell,

Who can describe the depth, length, and height of the void that has been left in my soul since you went to be with the Lord four years ago? The day you left, July 24, 2014, changed my life forever. My Love for you is as wide, long and high as the void that I am not able to escape every day that I breathe without you. The human mind alone is not able to comprehend this mystery called death. There is nothing that could have prepared me for losing you. The absence of your paramount presence in our lives sometimes causes anxiety and has caused me many sleepless nights. I cannot flee from the depth of my love for you – there is no escaping the wonderful memories that we created together. I have always stood in awe of your relationship with your God; it seemed that all you had to do was to express your heart to Him and He would move on your behalf.

I was often amazed as I watched you pray to God throughout your lifetime and witnessed Him answer your prayers, even when you felt you didn't deserve His grace. Your love for Him as your Father and His love for you as His son strengthened my faith. My heart sank as you prayed to God and expressed to Him how tired you had become as your health declined. When you asked Him to bring you home because your health was failing, your integrity compromised and your very profound intellect waned; I knew that He would grant your request. After you left, life became devoid of any meaning. I have yet been able to understand how the emotions of love, happiness, and joy that plagued my spirit with despair have remained the same emotions that bring me ultimate hope when I think of our lives together. For a brief second, I asked God, "What do I have to live for now?" The loneliness that I feel without you goes beyond the deepest part of the ocean. And, missing you is an understatement.

Our home is not the same, and the stillness and quietness are unbearable. Someone put it this way, "Grief is the loudest silence that I have ever heard." Having to live without your affirmation and validation has left me questioning my identity and femininity, and I feel insecure in so many areas. I did not realize how deeply connected we were spiritually and what an integral and essential role you played in my life. Widowhood has resurfaced every fiber of rejection that I felt as a child. In many ways, I have felt like a "second-class citizen." I have longed for your companionship; I miss our extensive and insightful conversations; I am lost not having you in church with me, I miss us working on committees together, the social life that we had with friends and every facet of life that we shared together. I will never forget the exciting vacations that we took with the children and the special romantic getaways that we took alone. It brought so much joy to me that you loved planning each one that we took for the 34 years that we were together. The last vacation that you planned for my birthday to Newport Beach, California in November 2013 was one that I shall never forget. Living without you is sometimes so painful.

I feel like a part of me is missing and adjusting to life without you seems like an injustice. It takes so much courage to socialize with friends that we fellowshipped with as a couple. I am thankful to God that I have such a strong and genuine relationship with Him. He has continued to carry me through this journey. Without you, Burrell, I have had to redefine myself as a woman, mother, and friend. This "new normal" and accepting this new role as a "widow" has caused so many emotions to surface. Some say that I have embraced the "widow label" well and brought life to it. But they don't know how hard it's been for me. I've kept going because I know that you would want me to. For 2 ½ years, I have hardly slept and almost suffocated during the nights from the anxiety of you not lying next to me in bed. The thought of not having you to solve the daily business matters with your eminently intellectual gift for reasoning, wisdom and sound judgment is simply scary and leaves me feeling so helpless and indecisive. How did you carry on the business so easily? Oh, how I miss the comforting sound of your very distinct bass voice; I miss the smell of your fine colognes in the mornings, your explicit sense of style, the suits that you wore, watching you get dressed in the mornings, the sound of your footsteps and the smell of your coffee brewing at five o'clock in the morning, your many calls to me throughout the day.

Our home is just a house now. The first three years, I was only thriving and not surviving in our home. I was terrified of being at home alone. Not only is your presence missed by me; but our children have been gravely impacted and affected by your absence. The very essence of the man that you were is missed. Your awesome and effortless leadership in our home as a father and husband, the security that you provided has left us seeking direction, and each of us is trying to find our own way individually. They live in the legacy that you left. Kali, Jhmeid, Burrell, Wesley, and Joel speak fondly of the love that they have for you and very often, they reminisce about the good times that they had when you took them to Braves, Hawks and Falcons games, the Peachtree Plaza as children and young adults. The many birthday parties that we planned for them created indelible memories in their hearts. They miss you so much, especially during the football and baseball seasons. You took your role so seriously as a father, your involvement in their lives when they were in elementary and high school, your involvement in PTA and so many other memories are priceless.

Taking them to the doctor when they were children was such a rarity with fathers; the doctors were so impressed with how involved you were as a dad, and they were impressed with your knowledge of their medical history. So few children have had or will have the experience of having a man like you as a father. In my opinion, you have exceeded and excelled above them all. The life lessons that they gained from us has produced five respectful, intelligent, compassionate, loving, and hardworking children with exceptional work ethics and morals.

All of them often express how they wish that you were here to give them advice; Jhmeid, and Kali who are now Directors and Project Managers in their professions long for your advice and sound judgment when challenges arise and; they miss your talks about politics and world issues, especially now given the controversial topics that have plagued our society. Jhmeid and Carlene, our wonderful Daughter In Love creates such a wonderful and pleasant atmosphere in their beautiful home. Our beautiful Daughter Kali, lives in the heart of Chicago in a luxury high rise condominium. She still manages employees here in Atlanta. I love going to visit her. She is a wonderful aunt and a wonderful daughter; she is very sensitive to my needs, but she works so very hard and dedicates much of her time to her profession. I'm still praying for her to get married, she deserves happiness and a husband to treasure her like you.

You would be so proud of Burrell III who is now married and is the Youth Pastor at Ray of Hope Christian Church. He attends Interdenominational Theological Center, studying for his Masters of Divinity; he is brilliant and academically astute. You also now have a new grandson who will carry on your legacy as "Burrell IV." Wesley and Mamiya have a wonderful marriage; they both have excellent jobs with the Federal

Government as Analytical Processors, and Wesley has certainly followed in your footsteps as a husband who loves and provides for his wife. He is an impeccable husband; very committed. He's still your analytical son and is a very meticulous man. People often comment that he has more of your looks and mannerisms than his brothers. They have created a wonderful home. I love Mamiya dearly. Joel has found his love. He is working as a missionary at Camp Cedine Bible Camp and as the Head Equestrian Trainer. He is hard working and still possesses that practical mind, tenacity, and zest for life that you often admired. Your loving grandchildren, Jhalen, Jhasmine, and Anjhel, have your precious memories to cherish. The special times that you spent with Jhalen are so precious to him, and he has so much respect for you as his grandfather. He is in college, exhibiting that Billingslea intellect, mature well beyond his age. He is majoring in Urban Planning and Development. The ones that you did not meet, Preston, Logon and now Burrell IV, who will carry on your name will never have a chance to meet the extraordinary and genius man that you were physically. But we will make sure that we will create traditions to honor and celebrate your life and share poignant memories with them that will keep your spirit alive so that they will be able to imagine what type of man their grandfather was. Our friends at church and the workforce community still comment on the phenomenal man that you were and the extremely impactful contributions that you made to the people whom you served and those who were involved with your work in the workforce industry. The men still talk about how they miss you calling them on the phone saying, "My Dear Brother." The church misses your impeccable leadership. There has not been another man who could gather men together for a cause like you. You were truly a "man's man," you were your brother's keeper. Those who were part of the Men's Fellowship Committee still comment on your humor and wit. And, they fondly remember your humor during the Support Services meetings. I still meet people who remember the profound impact that you made on their lives. You were such a humble man.

WHEN I KNEW THAT I LOVED YOU

I will never ever forget the lasting impression that you had on me as I sat in your Minorities in American History class at Atlanta Metropolitan College in 1977. I was so infatuated by your knowledge, your style of teaching and your exceptional intellect. You gave me a very insightful perspective on the Black experience. Although you graduated from Yale University with a degree in Philosophy and Urban Studies, and an IQ that gained you notoriety in Mensa, your swag, and your genuine and kind personality were intriguing. I fell in love with you, and I knew that I had to marry you. My mother loved you dearly, and I respected the love that you had for her. She thought you were a wonderful man and advised me that the love that you had for Kali and Jhmeid was admirable and was an attribute that was needed in a future husband. My family loved you and my sister profoundly and explicitly expresses that you were the first man that treated her like a lady and actually cared about her as a person. When I married you on September 27, 1980, it was the happiest day of my life. I considered it an honor to be married to you. I did not want to part with the essence of who you were. Your grandson, Jhalen, described you this way. He said, "My granddad is a simple but complex man." What a perfect way to describe you? I lived with you for 35 years. Our five children strive to live up to your legacy and make you proud. Being your wife is one role that I am so proud of and one of the greatest accomplishments that I've had. I've met so many women who did not have the "prize" that I had in a husband like you. I will always cherish our relationship, and the memories are far too many to forget. Many people have said that you spoiled me, but my response is that you took your role as a husband very seriously. You provided everything that our children and I needed. Your ability to save and grocery shop is still a mystery to me. Stockpiled pantry, every bill paid on time, cars paid for and serviced timely, home warranties on every appliance, vacations planned and paid for, romantic dinners planned, flowers sent just because you loved me, beautiful cards for every occasion, the many telephone calls throughout the day just to say, "I Love You," monthly stipends when I stopped working and stayed home to assist you while you were recuperating, clothes purchased because you wanted me to feel good about my appearance, beautiful rings and jewelry to show how much you cared; to name just a few. But most of all, your love, admiration, and protection are the things that I long for and miss the most. I will never forget the blessing that you bestowed on me before you left. "Janice," you stated, "your faithfulness has only been surpassed by God Himself," is what you said to me two months before your transition. How unselfish; what Love to bestow upon me. I was blessed with the apotheosis of a great gentleman, husband, and father. I am grateful and thankful that we were married for thirty-four years. Each day was a different experience. I will forever cherish the times that I had with you. I had my 60th birthday last year and had a party that I planned myself, oh, how I missed your presence and your impeccable planning skills. But I have used everything that I have learned from you. I had 90 guests who came to share dinner with me at Green Manor.

I am finally growing up; you would be proud of me. I am also a cancer survivor. I longed for you to be with me as I went through that journey. God took me through it. I had eight weeks of radiation. And I am Cancer Free today. But our son, Jhmeid, who has moved into his role as the Patriarch of this family, took the lead, each one of our children did their part in ensuring that I was cared for. I stayed in his home. He and Carlene, our dear daughter in love, provided excellent care for me. You would have been proud of them. We were a great team as parents, as you would say and it was evident in their actions. Although the continuous impact of grief for losing you is always with me, I am encouraged because resurrection is birthed in my soul daily. My inner spirit is renewed day by day. Somehow, I represent you still, and the light of your love is reflective in my spirit which creates a glow on the outside. You were such an integral and paramount part and the central aspect of my Life. My spirit longs for the support, love, and admiration that you expressed to me and I am sure that this void cannot be filled, neither can the thirst of your presence be quenched by anyone again. If I could make sure that you knew one thing, it would be for you to know that I was honored to serve you when you became ill; it was never a bother for me. It was my reasonable service because I knew in my heart that you would have done the exact thing. God gave me the spirit of compassion for you, and it carried me as I carried you.

God has given me three perspectives on this journey of grief: Wilderness, Wandering and Worshipping. I began in the wilderness; I did not know which way to turn until I began to abide in the secret place of the Most High. I wandered without any real purpose in life until my hope in God was refreshed by His word. He became my God of Hope. I have returned to the Heart of Worship, and my heart is learning to sing again. I celebrate your life, Burrell C. Billingslea, and I will always have you in the center of my Heart. I love you even more in your death. You were a paramount part of my Past, but you are also a spiritual Force in My Future! This is my tribute to You, Burrell. Goodbye, for now, my Love!

THE DAY AFTER YOU LEFT
Rosalind E. Bishop

Good morning, Dave:

It is the day after you left and I'm not quite sure what to say. I am at a loss for words, thoughts, and emotions. I am numb. I'm not sure how we got here. From a full life of love, joy, unity, and co-creating, how did we get here? Where are we? What happened to us?

Life was just a few faults short of perfect. We shared twenty-five years of our lives together. You were the love of my life since I was a teenager and we were the very best of friends. You were the epitome of a boyfriend, husband, and father of our children. Being so young (16) when we met, I never had the opportunity to wish for a better husband and father to my future family. God just chose to bless me with 25 years of you, and for that I am grateful.

Waking up to the reality that you are no longer physically with me is my best description of death, coming from someone who is yet to experience transition. I never knew what death felt like until now. But I'm still here. How and why is that? How do I function being dead but still breathing? How am I supposed to live let alone breathe without you? How do I raise our five children without you? I can't do this! I want to come where you are. Where are you, Dave?"

Grace is six years old now. Time flies, yet it stands still at the same time. It was just yesterday when you left and she was only 30 days old. Alaynah just turned 10, and can you believe Darius is 17 and about to graduate from High School? Daniel turned 21 and just returned home from a career experience in Los Angeles. Yeah, Daniel, who would have ever imagined? David is twenty-three and graduated from Morehouse College last month. I am honored and grateful to be the mother of your offspring, but I wasn't supposed to do this by myself. That was never the deal.

I managed to complete my master's degree. I decided to go back a year after you left to keep from being idle. I also completed all of my doctoral coursework and should be walking down the aisle in cap and gown in the spring of 2019. I had to keep going, Dave. I didn't know what to do without you, so I decided to invest in myself in order to keep going for our children. They have inspired me not just to live, but to continue thriving even while carrying the weight of my broken heart. They are the reason why I'm still here because most days, I still much rather be where you are.

I've preserved and protected my heart, soul and physical body since you left. I had no desire to be with anyone emotionally or intimately. It was never a thought until just over a year ago when Stanley came into my life. We met on a dating site, which you of all people knew wasn't in my character at all. A dear friend encouraged me to give it a try. She was concerned that I was working so hard at taking care of the children and everybody else, but didn't have companionship and partnership for myself. I decided to give it a try and committed to a one-month subscription when I received a message from Stanley just hours after signing up. After spending countless hours talking to him over the phone (at times from the moment the girls fell asleep at night to sunrise) and spending time with him, I realized after five years I still had feelings and emotions and that I was still human existing in this physical world. As my feelings for Stanley became stronger, I started to feel guilt and discomfort which stemmed from the reality that I was falling in love with a man other than you. I felt in some ways like I was cheating on you. The whirlwind of emotions consumed me and has continued to affect my relationship with Stanley.

After learning that Stanley had a heart attack prior to the age of fifty and was still managing a heart condition, I honestly became fearful. I didn't want to fall in love and lose love again. Not yet. My mind couldn't handle the thought. I tried to pull away, but the more I resisted, the more I desired to be with him. So, I decided to put my fears aside and love his healing heart back to life. As of today, I don't quite know where our relationship is headed, but I must admit to you that I love him and I feel in my soul that you are at peace with that.

I decided to write this letter to you today because I feel that it's time to release the hold I have on us and let the memories we created be just that, memories (fond reflections of life past). Holding on to us as we existed is only keeping me from fully being present in the moment. You were such an in-the-moment type of person, and I always admired that about you. You found joy and shed love, light, and laughter on every situation, no matter the severity of the circumstance. You were a fearless man who lived in confidence that God had your back if no one else. So, to honor you and the love we created and shared, I release us as we were and open my arms to fully embrace the future, both the joy and the lessons it may bring. I will no longer resist the opportunity to make new memories, understanding that my journey on this earth still continues until some unknown moment.

I look forward to catching up with you in the heavenly realm (when it's my turn) and reflecting on the gift of life we shared here in the physical world. It was all clearly an experience we were blessed to have along our eternal journeys.

As I write this letter, there are three birds flying about freely, yet, in unison. I take it as a message from God that it is OK to live and love without reserve. You nor God will judge me on how and whom I chose to live forward with in the rest of my days. Both of you only desire for me to love and be loved. My concern of not being faithful to you was just released in one long exhale as I watch these three birds fly together gracefully. I am assured that whomever I share the rest of my days with was already connected to this journey.

It was only yesterday that you left so, I'm OK with waiting until tomorrow to see you again. Soar in bliss, my love, I've released the weight I've had on us in this physical experience, and I vow that I too will soar through this life in peace, love, joy, and light.

Until tomorrow.

Your eternal soulmate,
Roz

TIMELESS LOVE THAT ENDURES
Johnny Causey

My story began in the fall of 2000, in the town of Millington, TN, around October 19th. I was working for the Navy Locator at the time. One day, as I was returning from lunch, and walked into my work area, I found this young (Aquilla Jones) lady making copies. As she finished her task, she accidentally dropped her papers on the floor. I did the noble thing that I was accustomed to doing. I bent down and helped her gather her papers into an organized stack. She gave me a huge infectious smile and said: "He helped me!!" It was at that moment that her accent stunned me. I was smitten by her voice and kind ways. After that, I asked everyone I met about the Jamaican Lieutenant, but no one knew whom I was talking about. The humorous side of the story was that she was trying to find out who the Jamaican was as well because her coworkers were asking her. I did not realize that she worked right across the hall from me. After all the looking and searching, I found out where her office was located and decided to stop by. It was then that I found out that she wasn't from Jamaica, but from Charleston, SC. She also realized that she was, in fact, the mysterious Jamaican Lieutenant. Our courtship started a week after that, and we were married four months later on April 13, 2001. Good Friday. Anyone who says that Friday the 13th is a bad luck day doesn't know of the Blessings of GOD, because I was truly blessed on that day. Aquilla was life to me, and considering the past so-called loves, nothing compared to her.

In September 2001, a tragedy struck the nation, and Aquilla, (Q) as all knew her by, deployed to Bahrain. I could not imagine how we could be separated at such an amazing time in my life. She had opened up a part of me that I had not known was there. She was gentle, sweet, loving, and kind to all she came in contact with. A magnificent social butterfly. She gave to anyone in need, no matter the circumstance. I was floored by the mere fact that someone could be so genuine and real. On November 4, 2001, I stepped foot in Bahrain, and thus began the love of a lifetime for us. Our first two years of marriage were spent in the country of Manama, Bahrain. That was where we formed a bond of Love, Togetherness, and True Devotion. This was a fairytale, as so many people there told us that they sought the love that we shared. I could not fathom the love that grew from those two years of being in a country so far away that was enchanting as well as mysterious to our families. I always said to people when they asked about our life together, that I had the fairytale life, fairytale wife, and the fairytale Love, with the most amazing bride that I could ever imagine!!

Q taught me how to love by the way she loved others. She taught me how to give to no end, as well as be a blessing to all those I came in contact with. She was a teacher, a wife, a Lady, and an Officer that was never too high to get dirty and work with those whom she served with. We traveled and blessed people wherever we went. Sometimes I wondered where we got the endless supply of things we had and acquired. But I understood that no matter how much you give away, GOD always refills your barn.

At that time, with all the love we shared, I thought I knew what love was, but, boy, I was in for a shock. Fast-forward to May 2013. We were now stationed in Great Lakes, IL, and Q was a Commander. I flew to Niagara Falls, and she took a Mega Bus to Millington, TN, for a Senior Officer's Human Resource Course. She loved the Mega Bus. I never liked the idea of us traveling apart, and never in two different directions. As I was attending a Commencement Ceremony, and had no reception on the border, little to my knowledge, calls were coming to my phone in volumes. I didn't receive any of the calls until I got to the Niagara Air Base. The messages were saying that she was rushed to the Baptist Hospital in Memphis. I called our friends that lived in the city that I was in and left my car and everything I had there.

Although it was Mother's Day, I caught a flight and landed in Memphis to be with my beloved Q. As I walked into the door of the hospital room, she lit up so bright in amazement, but she was very weak and seemingly frail. I held her and stayed with her, by her bedside.

Noticing that she had lost a lot of weight, and was acting very sluggish, I asked the nurse what type of medication she was on to make her this way. I immediately asked her to change to lighter medicine for the pain. The next morning, Q was chipper, and we began the journey of "Timeless Love."

Here was the woman that I cherished and adored, lying in the hospital. I was very disappointed with myself for not being able to protect her from this dreaded sickness that somehow attacked her body. On May 21, 2013, the doctor gave us the diagnosis of **Adenocarcinoma of an Unknown Primary**, and although difficult to believe, the journey of Timeless Love began. Q and I loved like there was no tomorrow. Although she was being victimized by this disease, I stood beside her to carry out her wishes, as well as being her legs and strength. Many disappointments came along the way, but it is now that I understand it all. She was holding on for me. The love that she gave me as well as showing me how to express my love, and promising to love whomever I chose as she transitioned to rest. We prayed for healing, but it came not on this side, but on Eternity's side. She transitioned in my arms with a smile. Yes, "Timeless Love" because although she transcended to her time, she equipped me to be able to love someone as she loved me, THEREBY HER LOVE ENDURES THROUGH TIME...

PLANTING SEEDS
Franda Clay

My dear, sweet, darling – Jay,

The day I met you, I didn't know how much my world would change. I just knew that God had planted someone very special in my life. With you, I got to see new things from your perspective, and we had so many adventures together. I experienced life in the arms of someone that I loved and trusted from the very first day. When I think about how young we were, it seems like it was almost too young to know what true love meant. Yet, despite everything, we took a chance. We vowed to make this life work until our dying days. Amid all our fears and reservations, you promised that you would never leave. I promised you that I would always love you. So, we rode off into the sunset to begin a new adventure called life. You planted the seeds, and I nurtured them.

We built a home and raised our daughters to love each other unconditionally just as we did each other. We cherished our home with laughter and memories that have lasted a lifetime. You made sure that we were protected from all harm, well taken care of, comfortable, and loved. You showed our daughters what it was like to fall in love with a man and to be loved by a man. You taught me how to be strong and fierce so that the world could not take advantage of me. We taught you the true meaning of love and how to open your heart. We became YOUR girls. You planted the seeds, and I nurtured them.

So, when God called you home, I didn't know what to think. My mind went blank. When a sense of reality returned, all I could think about were the plans we were making to expand our family. We wanted to grow old together. I hadn't imagined life without you, and you couldn't see living without me. Then, I thought about our girls. My body went cold at the thought of them not having you in their lives. It was like you died all over again when I had to tell them what happened. I will never forget saying the words, "Daddy isn't coming home." The piercing screams and shattered dreams were too much for such young babies to experience. I held them extra tight every night because I didn't want them to feel what I felt. I only wanted them to feel that you hadn't left them. You planted the seeds, and I nurtured them.

Then time moved on, and life resumed, but it wasn't the same without you. We leaned on one another for support as our healing process began. Three moving as one – minus one. We each cried and tried to hide the pain of missing you. Over time, we reminisced to the point where it no longer hurt to bring up all your antics that constantly kept us laughing. We always wondered how you would be today and what you might say to keep us laughing. Our relationship became a bond to keep us strong, and to get us through losing you. What almost destroyed us then, has made us unbreakable now. You planted the seeds, and I nurtured them.

Now it's been more time and talks, more laughter, and more life. The healing has continued. We talk about you as though you are still here; lingering in the atmosphere and watching over us like you always have been. So now you can see that they are no longer the little girls you left behind missing their daddy. They are beautiful young women; still missing their daddy. Both are a special part of you, and both have your sense of humor and intellect. They aspire to be an extension of you, and both want nothing more than to make you proud of them. They still look at you as their hero and first love. You planted the seeds, and I nurtured them.

Now I understand that although it wasn't our plan; it was God's plan. When you took my hand and promised to never leave, you kept that promise. You planted two beautiful daughters in my life. You planted a stable home for us; you planted dreams and goals for us. You gave us the security to make it in this world. You planted all the love a man could give his family into our hearts. I never realized until now that your purpose was to plant the seeds of abiding love. Once that task was complete, it was my turn to nurture. So, you never left. You abided with us. You planted the seeds, and I nurtured them.

As I look at the daughters we have raised, I see you in them. The seeds you planted blossomed into two beautiful young women who know what it's like to be loved by a man. They want nothing more than to make you happy and proud of them. It's remarkable, how strong, independent, intelligent, successful, and sweet they are. When people compliment me about them, I would like to take all the credit, but I can't. I know that I played a significant role, but I also know who planted those seeds. Without your love, they wouldn't be who they are today. You planted the seeds, and I nurtured them.

One day, they will make the same vow we did. They will find a man like you, fall in love, get married, have kids, and make plans to grow old together. They will take those seeds to start their own families, and they will nurture those seeds until it's time to leave this earth. So, you see, your vow and those seeds of abiding love you planted grew into healthy, happy young women ready to conquer the world. Someday, when I share my stories about you with our grandkids, they will laugh and ask me to tell them more about you. And I will tell them how I took the abiding love that you planted, and I nurtured them.

Every memory made with your spouse is a seed for the future. Time, love, family, friends, and commitment have nurtured those seeds so that someday, you will be surrounded by the garden of love the two of you planted.

I KNOW WHY THE RED BIRD COMES
Sonia Lynn Davis

Living with the death of my husband, Jake Davis, Jr. is by far one of the biggest hurdles I have had to face. At times, I feel such deep sadness. I constantly pray that my widowhood becomes a milestone on my road to continue life's journey. I also pray that each day without Jake will imperceptibly start to get better. It has been a slow and painful journey – a journey I didn't choose, but still a journey I must find the strength to continue. There are days when I don't exactly know how to carry on – but I know that with God all things are possible...

To reassure us of that, God often sends us a sign. In my case, the "red bird."

I am so thankful to have had 28 years of marriage with Jake. On December 31, 1988, we took vows of marriage after a two-year dating relationship. It was obvious that God had sent me a kind, patient, caring, loving, steadfast man of God. With a heart full of God's Word, Jake would proclaim, "He who finds a wife, finds a good thing," to which I would reply, "I'm the good thing." Our humor and balance made us exceptional company and perfect companions. Our family topped off with the birth of our one and only daughter, Amanda – the apple of both of our eyes.

As time passed and we entered seasons of reminiscing, Jake would remind me of how much his mother loved the "red bird." That's why after her passing, he would point out the many times a lone red bird was spotted near our home. It became our seemingly light-hearted acknowledgment that his mother was checking on us.

On December 21, 2016, Jake joined his mother in Heaven. Less than 24 hours after Jake's passing, the Lord sent a baby blanket to help dry our tears with the birth of our first grandchild, Faith – named for Jake's most notable attribute. Faith served as a sweet reminder of God's love as we grieved the loss of her granddaddy just hours before her arrival.

There are many memories of my relationship with Jake that linger in my mind. I grew to love him in so many ways. I found a great soul, a gentleman that I liked as much as I loved and a man that I trusted wholeheartedly and emotionally during our marriage. He displayed that I had his heart and bonded with me for life. Jake was loyal and faithful, and I always felt that he worked to please me the best way he knew how. His love made me feel secure and content.

Jake took an active interest in the well-being, personal growth, spiritual nurturing and support of all that made contact with him. It was obvious that he loved the Lord, his family, and friends. In 2010, Jake was ordained a deacon in our church, New Testament Gospel Worldwide Ministries, where he served faithfully. Even when not well, he pressed his way to both the 9:30 a.m. and 11:00 a.m. services often being the first to stand during praise and worship – singing loudly and boldly – notes that only the Lord Himself could discern but reflecting a deeply personal and true heart for prayer, praise, and worship. Jake's faithfulness extended to his last employer of 10 years, Jonesboro High School. He proudly supported the school's faculty, staff, students and sports teams – with an extra special place in his heart for the boys' basketball team. Perhaps the "red bird," in this case the school's Cardinal mascot, added to his love for the school.

Jake received a stage 4 liver cancer diagnosis three years before his passing. Even his doctors took hold of his testimony that he "didn't walk in his diagnosis" – instead, he "walked in faith." While he was thankful for the available treatments and wisdom of the doctors, his ultimate faith was in his belief that "The Lord is in control" – the phrase he even quietly whispered over the phone to our laboring daughter in his final days with us here on the earth.

Jake truly knew that the Lord was in control. Still, he didn't leave all the work to the Lord. He covered our family daily with prayers and declarations detailed in his prayer journal. To read through his large, leather-bound journal full of his single-spaced, handwritten notes and prayers is truly a gift that keeps on giving. Page after page – the journal is a true testament to how Jake walked in faith. The journal reflects much of his own journey, but sacrificially not with prayers primarily for himself – but for his family. In reading the many passages in the journal, it's clear that he was preparing himself (and us) to know that God's plan is sovereign.

A few weeks after Jake passed, I heard a familiar tapping near the window. However, this time Jake wasn't there to share in the novelty of our visiting red bird. Sometimes we spotted the red bird which usually arrived unannounced. Other times, a tapping sound would get our attention outside of the window where we'd see a few birds – and among them often the lone red bird, frolicking.

But this time when I looked, I noticed the usually lone red bird wasn't alone. There were TWO red birds. With an overwhelming sense of peace and joy, I truly believe that God was showing me that Jake was now assigned to "check on us."

Several of my family members and friends know the story of the red bird. We are amazed at how often we see the red bird – even "out of season"— and it brings a smile to all our faces.

As the Lord gives me the strength to carry on – that strength is fueled by the red bird who pops by periodically. Sometimes the red bird seems to appear out of nowhere. Sometimes the red bird follows me into uncharted territory. And sometimes the red bird taps. The red bird is a true symbol of our "Abiding Love," with feelings and memories that last forever.

No matter how it appears, the red bird gives me a sense of peace (and at times even humor) when it shows up. It gives me the confirmation that all things are possible when I look to God. In fact, I don't see the red bird when I'm looking down – only when I'm looking up... and often when I'm looking forward.

Yes, I know why the red bird comes.

GOD'S GIFT TO ME
Keith Horton

On a Saturday evening in February 1988 at Fort Stewart Georgia, I met the woman that would change my life forever. We met at a fashion show, and on June 10, 1989, we married. Lisa was God's gift to me. He gave me my soul mate, my biggest supporter and my spiritual mate. We grew up 150 miles from each other in South Georgia. Our parents were educators; our fathers graduated from Tennessee State and were both Alphas. Lisa earned a basketball scholarship, and I earned a football scholarship to college. We both grew up in the church, and although we worshipped at different denominations, she made a family decision that we would worship together. She sacrificed her way of worship, and I am forever grateful for her willingness to keep us together in everything that we did.

Lisa and I were blessed with a daughter and a son whom we cherish. In October 1993 and February 1994, tragedy rocked our world; our fathers passed away three months apart. Two men whom we adored were gone so quickly and so young. Lisa was my sounding board and biggest supporter during my military career. She selflessly took on the role of a military wife and contributed greatly to our family as a very diversified hardworking educator, daycare director, coach, and loving wife.

The winter of our union began in March 2013 as I was thanking and praying to God for what he had done in our lives. I asked Him for more responsibility and to expand our boundaries. Lisa earned her doctorate in education in 2010 and wanted to put it to use but never seemed to get that promotion. God answered our prayers, but it wasn't the way that I envisioned. On 29 March 2013, Lisa informed me that during her annual checkup, the doctor noticed some lumps in her breast. Later that week, we received the dreadful news that she had an aggressive type of breast cancer. We prayed! The faith that she had in God kept her in the right mindset and spirit. Lisa immediately began chemotherapy and radiation treatments. Within a few weeks, her hair began to shed. Near the end of the month, Lisa informed me with excitement that she was offered the Athletic Director position. She was determined to defeat this dreadful disease and at the very least, walk this journey with faith, courage, and dignity.

At this very time, my walk with God grew greater, and my love and respect for this awesome woman of God grew exponentially. A few weeks later, I was offered a dream job by the Governor's executive staff. On Memorial Day, we made a decision to shave her head so that we were both bald. I will never forget going to the grocery store and watching her strut across that store like she had a head full of hair. There were at least two men who stopped her and said, "Thank you so much... I am going to tell my wife that it's OK." Lisa and I decided that we were not going to allow this disease to make us shameful. She was not going to be shameful for something that was out of her control, and I was not going to be ashamed of what the disease did to her outer body. God is faithful! We started our new jobs on 1st July, 2013. Lisa excelled as a teacher, coach, and athletic director and in November, she underwent a double mastectomy. I loved Lisa even more for her courage and strength even though the disease changed her outward appearance. I thought we were done with the surgeries and the effects of this disease but in April 2014, I almost lost her to an aneurysm as cancer had spread to her brain. She had emergency surgery and stayed in ICU for only four days.

With God's grace, she walked out of ICU on a Thursday and the next day we were on the road to attend our daughter's college graduation. Lisa persevered through it all without a mumbling word, demonstrating the faith and strength she received from God. I was so proud of her leading by example, working every day, ministering to others and always maintaining a loving disposition. God later blessed us with a son-in-law, daughter-in-law and gave Lisa what she always wanted; grandchildren (3). By January 2015, her health began to decline, Lisa was limited to a wheelchair or walker; she still worked, coached and attended church. In March 2015, I received a phone call from the doctor stating that after examining her, it appeared the cancer had spread to her lungs. I immediately left work and raced to the doctor's office. When I got there, Lisa had been wheeled outside. When I saw her, she smiled and said: "I guess we're going to have to go to Plan B." I was awed by her disposition and even more determined to love her to my fullest ability. Over the next two years, it was my honor to take care of her; I dressed and undressed her for work, helped her bathe, cooked and maintained the house. I was honored to be in her presence as I knew that she was demonstrating Godliness in the most unusual circumstances. Although Lisa was outfitted with a pump to remove fluid from her lungs, she kept it moving, teaching, coaching and churching all the way until 9 December 2017. Lisa was admitted to the hospital for stomach pain, and on 12 December, the doctors informed us that her transition was imminent. In Lisa's own way and without a tear, she stated, "I knew this day would come." The next morning, the Lord's angels carried her to his bosom. On her headstone, it reads, "No individual has any right to come into the world and go out of it without leaving behind him distinct and legitimate reasons for having passed through it" ...Lisa left a legacy.

TIL THE WHEELS RUN OFF!
Veronica Lewis

How many of us can say they married and lost the love of their life not once but twice? It's a question that makes me smile, yet at the same time, it causes tears to stream down my face. You see, I'm one of those seemingly cursed, yet actually blessed ones. Let me tell you why.

By the time Steven decided to give me anything more than a passing glance, I'd been in love with him for 4 years! The years following would be ebb and flow... ebb and flow. Though childhood sweethearts, it was many moons later, after two children and marrying that we would find out he had a serious medical condition. And it would be too late to really enjoy each other as we had pledged in our vows. He was very ill. After many years of doctor's visits and long hospital stays, he succumbed to complications arising from his illness. Death was not something we thought about at our young age. The shock and dismay of losing him was overwhelmingly devastating. It was 1984, and grief counseling was unheard of in my circle. So,

I struggled and prayed, struggled and prayed and so did our young sons.

But then, there was you! My Beloved Rudy!

"You!" I turned slowly as this voice vibrated throughout the store. Our eyes instantly locking on each other and in that moment, that split second, I realized this stranger was pointing at me! You shouted across the room, "YASSIR! YOU ARE MINE!" Laughing to myself, I thought, "This guy is insane!" That big white, all 32 bright shining smile of yours was all I saw as you pushed your way through the turnstile straight toward me! And it was all I would ever want to see for many years to come... At a time when I couldn't even breathe, God sent you "straight outta" Heaven! And it was then that our magic together began!

It was crazy! You looked like this guy I'd seen once in passing on the street! I had been in the car with my first husband and didn't want to stare at you. But he caught me and simply said, "That's a nice fella right there." Feeling guilty, I was like, "How do you know?" To which he replied, "I just know." And then there you were walking into my job and wait... were you stalking me.... putting your claim on me? HA! How could this be? Where did you come from? Is this real? You were so tall and lanky, pouncing on me before my mind could shout back the answers to all my questions. I noticed my boss counting the clock, so I snapped back to my assignment. Reacting quickly, I turned toward you, a dark and handsome stranger. "How can I help you?" "No help needed," you said because you had acquired all you needed to know about me from another source. I was in awe to think that you would even have me on your mind. Truly, you were the most "magnificent" man I'd ever seen or would care to see ever again.

But alas, life wasn't that simple, was it? I remember having to explain to you that I was married and that my husband was very sick. To my surprise, you didn't push me; you seemed to understand. That's when I first knew that besides the physical attributes, your mama had raised a really fine gentleman.

Months later Steven would pass away... sad times, incomprehensible times. Shortly thereafter, I saw one of the guys that initially came in with you. I always jokingly denied having sent him back to tell you that I was now a widow. Afraid that I had lost my "Magic Man," I poopooed all the noise in my ear that it was too soon. I felt that if I didn't act, I would never see you again and the thought of that crushed my soul. You took your precious time too before you called me! Lol! When you did, it was you confessing the two words I truly didn't want to hear. "I'm married." My heart sunk, I got this sickening feeling, and I think I hung up, I don't remember, lol. Persistency was the name of your game, and eventually, I listened to your side of the story. Wrong though it was, I gave in, and we began to see each other.

And we lived in that magnificent love for the next 32 years as man and wife. What lesson did I learn from you? From us? Well, after you left me, all the joys of you came back to haunt me, even now, almost 3 years later. I miss everything about you, not just physically but the total beauty of you! Through the countless and intimate talks we always had, you taught this "Paper Bag Brown," "Little Green Girl" all I needed to know about life. As the sun rose on March 5, 2016, you, my beloved husband, gently took your last breath. Once again, I was devastated, only differently this time. Before, with Steven, I was a scared child, but with you, I had become one strong lady!

One thing you taught me was how to live every day like it's my last because one day, sure enough, it will be. You took that million-dollar smile with you wherever you journeyed. Your testimony of recovering from drug use and infidelity spoke volumes of The Goodness of The Lord on every turn. Many were wowed by the change God allowed them to see in you. Was he perfect, you might ask? Of course, he wasn't! Was he perfect for me? Oh yes, he was! When others saw a guy that was wrong for me, my mind would always revert to what was really behind his magnificent smile. What lived there was an abiding love for God, for family and for me. Though my heart is broken and I miss you every second of each day, I have found comfort knowing that you truly loved me and everything about me. Heaven truly has become more attractive to me now because it is there that I will see you again. Love truly does live on in one's heart.

"Good Night, Irene!"

THE BLOOD OF MY ABIDING LOVE
Ebony Lewis-Hodge

To the Love of My Life Jamal Hisheam Hodge,

As I recall the first moment that we met, I'm reminded of the abiding love that you were determined to conquer. To give love and receive nothing but God's best of an honest, true love of a lifetime. It was a hot summer day on August 4, 2008, when you approached me at Marta's Dunwoody train station as we were both waiting for the southbound train after a long day at work. You confidently walked up to me and said, "You're wifey and don't even know it," and walked away. Those were your first words to me in which I was annoyed and politely ignored you.

When the train arrived, I sat and began gazing out of the window when you suddenly appeared again. This time sitting beside me facing the aisle while engaging in conversations with a colleague in the opposite seat across from you. As I began to eavesdrop, I heard an entrepreneurially minded man who was prophesying his business goals for an innovative IT consulting firm. The power, passion, and excitement to relentlessly pursue your dreams were so intriguing that I immediately interrupted your conversation requesting, "May I have a business card?" while handing you one of mine. At the time, I was a young CEO of my company who needed your services to program and update my company's website. We briefly discussed my needs until we departed for our various destinations. Although you called me the next day, I returned your phone call two days later in which I admired your professionalism and tenacity when you followed up. I hired and paid you for the project, but you rejected the payment and requested a date instead. I declined and wouldn't give you the time of day. Months went by, and you kept chasing me despite the numerous times I turned you down.

I finally gave in and met you again at the train station to take us to our first date, the laser show at Stone Mountain Park where we had real-life conversations. I saw a very vulnerable side of you... a broken man seeking God's heart, a visionary, an exceptional father who just wanted to win in life. First, a beautiful friendship developed between us in which we earned each other's trust, loyalty, and integrity to then becoming business partners, to finally each other's "King & "Queen"/Love of a Lifetime by saying "I do" on March 1, 2011.

No one understood our goals and dreams for life except for us, so we remained humble and diligent in the journey to prevent the many dream assassinators from defeating us. Our motto for our life was, "We WIN!" And we definitely won by leading an awesome family of 6 children, an amazing Marriage Ministry, thriving profitable businesses, and the ability to travel the world. Sometimes with just only us and sometimes the entire family. When I think about all of the memorable moments that we shared, I give God the honor, glory, and praises for the blessing you were to me. Nothing in life could've prepared me for Saturday, November 5, 2016. We started the day at church by leading our Marriage Ministry, and we were so excited that God chose us for the mission. You led in the prayer, and 14 couples answered the call to salvation and for a prosperous marriage. It was a fulfilling long day as we were completing Kingdom business. We were exhausted and went home. I just wanted to rest, but you left to go to the store.

As I was sleeping, I dreamed that you woke me up from my sleep. You were sitting on the edge of the bed. After shaking me urgently to get up, I got out of bed. We both stood up, and you grabbed my hand, looking me into my eyes filled with tears. I never saw you like that. You said, "Eb! I just want to let you know that I'm not coming home anymore, but God will take care of you and the children. I'm leaving for good, but I can't explain it right now." I became very angry, irate and screamed, "How dare you…? What do you mean? How do I tell the kids that you walked out on us? How are you going to walk out on me after we just had a great Marriage Ministry? What am I'm supposed to tell them? What's suddenly gotten into you?" We were both crying, and you wiped the tears from my eyes while trying to calm me down. You hugged me saying, "I love you!" and walked out of the bedroom. I was so confused, still screaming due to this sudden breakup.

All of a sudden, I woke up and realized I was dreaming. I looked at my phone and realized the time, and you were not back from the store. I called you, but the phone went straight to voicemail. I felt knots in my stomach, but I didn't know why. After lying in bed for a while waiting for you to get home, I was alerted by the doorbell on my phone and saw the Home surveillance system app of two policemen at our front door. I ran downstairs to answer the door, confused. The detectives began asking me lots of questions, "Are you, Ebony? Is this the home of Jamal Hodge? What's your relationship to him? Do you drive a white SUV? Does it have two car seats?" I frantically responded, "Where is Jamal? What do you want? Yes! I'm Ebony! Yes!!!! Jamal is my husband! Yes, he lives here! Yes! We have a white truck." She responded, "I'm sorry ma'am, but Jamal is deceased." I screamed in confusion to the top of my lungs, wishing this was just a nightmare. My raging screams and cries for help woke the kids and they came running down the stairs in confusion too. My uncontrollable cries had me numb, shocked, and lifeless.

They entered our home trying to control me. They began asking me questions regarding where you were going. I asked, "So where did the car accident happen? What hospital was he taken to?" They looked at each other and said, "He was shot." I panicked in disbelief all over again, screaming and feeling like it could not be happening. "Shot? No, God! How could this happen? Why, God? Why?"

As I'm healing from your unexpected demise, while seeking justice, truth, and healing, God has given me some amazing grace and strength that I never knew existed. My heart has been broken, and I see how the enemy tries to kill, steal, and destroy. In the fate of this tragedy, you were killed, our hopes and dreams were stolen, and our family was destroyed. But I also know we serve a good God who will never leave us or forsake us. I trust God that justice will prevail, dreams will flourish, and our family will be resurrected.

Jamal, I will forever be in debt to God that he chose me to give you abiding love of a lifetime. I will always love you constantly, now, forever, and always.

Love,

Your Queen, Your Fire

Ebony Lewis-Hodge

MEZ AND CANDY LOGAN'S
25 YEAR SECRET GARDEN
Daina Matheny Logan

I fell hard for my Navy Seal, crazy sexy cool, ooh he got good hair shag, devil jeans and speedo shorts wearing, incredible hulk Superman. The perfect teeth and smile that lights up the room. My freaky don't sleep with yo mouth open deliciousness snicker bar Leo lion. We had a 25-year honeymoon with the do not disturb sign, sipping on an adult beverage on deck. My Navy seal jumped out of a tree with a stick of gum to save our world for our family. I know with everything in me, GOD and my Navy Seal would not want me to grieve myself to death or defile my body. I now love and take care of me. I'm 40 pounds down. There is life after my storm, tornado and rain. I'm excited about sipping Pina Colada, getting caught in the rain, being 50 and fabulous, a child of God, King Jesus, and the Holy Spirit. Hello world, taste the rainbow through my life. I know with everything in me, everything and everyone is a precious gift. Candi Logan is a fine wine waiting on my well-done filet mignon to share my secret garden, making love between the sheets. Juicy fruit, funny how time flies when you're having fun, baby I want to do all of the things yo man can't do. Taste and see that the Lord is good. Chico stick, Prince.

Good morning My Chico Stick Prince, this is Candi Logan. I wanted to tell you Happy New Year. From what I see you appear to be a great guy with many personalities and layers, that I would love to slowly uncover as I peel mine back. Many times, I find myself thinking of you for no reason and laugh. I never in a million years would ever think I would have to start over getting to know others on a nonsexual way, dating or opening my heart with someone other than my husband. Giving my number out, made me feel like I was cheating on my husband of 25 years. I know that he would not want me to be alone, grieve myself to death or just defile my body. I am a woman that LOVE💜 GOD, Jesus and the HOLY SPIRIT. Not because of what I was told, not because what I read, but because at my lowest, loneliness, dirty and darkest hour, they whispered sweetness, and sweet somethings in my ear and my Soul. On the day's I didn't want to live, be a widow, a single parent, and an empty nester. While trying to protect and hold my family together. I am very passionate and protective with pure rawness right now. I will be so pleased to meet you.

CANDI has left the building...Peace, love and hair grease.

Two important lessons learned:
- Love is precious and should never be taken for granted.
- Tell and show your spouse often that you love them.

TRUE LOVE NEVER DIES
FORGIVENESS, LOVE, AND HELLO
Patricia Rivas

April 1994. That was the month, and year my life changed forever with these few words, "I'll forgive you, if you allow me to take you out." I was unaware at the time that the fine, handsome, young, man, with the infectious smile speaking those words, would sweep me off my feet, becoming my best friend, husband, lover, soul mate, and father of my beautiful children. Chad's unconditional love towards me changed me and my life forever.

Me, 24, just a few months' shy of my twenty-fifth birthday. Him, 26, caramel complexion, broad shoulders, contagious smile, dimples, oozing swag, and very easy on the eyes! I was reluctant a few days earlier to give him the time of day and my telephone number when he inquired. So reluctant to the extent that I was downright rude to him. Not because I was not interested. I was, but I recently had my heart broken by someone who truly did not appreciate or deserve my love. I was oblivious during our initial interaction, but God was going to use this very same man to vanquish all my thoughts and ideas that all men are dogs! This man was truly my gift from above. Custom made just for me, drawing me closer to the Lord, showing and filling me with agape love, propelling me into my destiny.

Forgiveness:

A friend of mine witnessed it all. She persisted that I call him and apologize for being so rude. Two days later, I relented to her request. I picked up the office phone dialing the extension for the Bio-Medical department. After a brief hold, he answered with that same cheery voice. I could hear him smiling thru the phone. I spoke, saying, "I know you do not know who this is," but before I could finish, he responded saying, "oh, but I do," and he proceeded to say my name. My once professional voice softened, my shoulders relaxed, and butterflies began to flutter in my stomach. I slowly began to apologize for my behavior, but he would not let me off the hook so easily. He was so cool and downright smooth with how he handled my weak and feeble attempt to apologize and end the call quickly. He took his time, made me squirm, and then he spoke those simple words, "I'll forgive you if you allow me to take you out"? Time stood still; the only audible sounds were my heavy breathing and the rumbling in the pit of my stomach. Yes, my barely whispered response.

Schedules checked, plans made, two months later, the first date. By the time dinner at Bennigan's Restaurant was done, I felt like I reconnected with an old friend. No awkwardness. We were both extremely relaxed as if we had known each other all of our lives. The conversation was titillating and at times downright hypnotic. It could have continued all night, but the plan after dinner was to see the movie Crooklyn at the AMC

Theater. There was no denying the great chemistry between us! It was too obvious to be ignored. The connection on our first date was downright palpable; all of our senses engaged and heightened. The only light flooding the room came from the movie screen, he gently reaches for my hand, I instinctively extend my hand toward his. Our fingers instantly entwine, visible sparks fly, it feels comfortable, right, and safe, like home. I knew at that moment this beautiful soul was my Boaz, my forever.

Fast-forward one and a half years later. Whirlwind romance, pre-Christmas dinner and the perfect marriage proposal at Benihana's Restaurant. Suddenly I turn and look, and he is next to me down on one knee. I start to cry; he is misty-eyed; he gently wipes my tears with soft finger strokes. He professes his everlasting love for me. He reminds me that he knew from the moment he first saw me, that I was the one he would spend the rest of his life with sharing dreams, love, and children. He promises to always cherish me and our love. Me sobbing YES! He pulls me up and into his broad chest encircling loving arms around me. He tilts my tear stained face towards his, plants a sweet, gentle kiss on my lips and places the ring on my finger! Loud thunderous applause, more tears, lingering kisses, tighter embraces, and lots of I love you.

Love:

We professed our love in front of God, family, and friends on a Saturday afternoon. The clouds were dark as a heavy, constant rain fell a few hours before the wedding ceremony was to begin. I start to cry because no bride expects rain on her wedding day. A wise woman in the room says a few words that calm and center me, bringing a smile to my face. She says the rain is falling because God above is happy we found each other and are marrying on this day. All the angels in heaven are rejoicing, and the rain is their tears overflowing because of the forthcoming union. Suddenly, I do not mind the rain, but as soon as I'm okay with it, the rain stops and the clouds part ushering in beautiful sunshine and a vibrant 3D appearing rainbow over the wedding venue.

Chad and I had a beautiful marriage rooted and grounded in the Lord. We loved hard, wide, and deep never allowing a day or an opportunity to pass without confessing and expressing our love and mutual respect for each other. My husband was my biggest cheerleader and motivator, but he would also lovingly tell me when I was wrong. He encouraged me never to settle, always to do and be my best, reaffirming his love for me daily and challenging me to spend daily quality time in the presence of the Lord. In our short 21.5 years together on this side, we were blessed with two beautiful and amazing children, gifts from God to raise and train up in the way they should go. Our children greatly enriched our lives, but we always carved out, what we called "us time." The amount of time or the destination did not matter, as long as we were together, doing what we enjoyed best, being in each other's presence talking, laughing, debating, crying, praying, singing, dancing, and being downright silly. It truly didn't matter what we were doing, as long as we did it together. Chad had the best sense of humor. He kept me in stitches. Quite often I would laugh so hard that tears would stream down my face, as I barely made it to the bathroom, trying not to wet myself. My husband was so easy to love because he possessed the biggest, most caring heart. He loved people, never met a stranger, everyone was his friend. He would give you the skin, marrow, and bone from his back, smiling that infectious smile the entire time, while speaking an encouraging and uplifting word from God. He was my ride and die, my confidant, my very best friend on this side, my lover and babies' daddy. He was faithful to God and his family until the very end, and I miss him more and more with each passing day.

Hello:

May 30, 2015, was a beautiful and picture-perfect Saturday morning. It is routine for us to stand in a circle and pray before we leave the house. My husband says to our son, "son, I want you to pray for your family today," and he prayed a mighty prayer to the Lord! Wonderful and fun-filled breakfast with the children, no drama! A short visit to Heaven's Lane (actual name of the street we were on), dropping off my car to the mechanic. My husband calls in to a 10 AM Elder's meeting, during the call I hear him say, "It's just another day in paradise." A quick stop at the store to pick up a gift for a graduation party my son was attending. He face times his favorite niece while I am in the store. A short stop to clean my husband's car, our children who are eight years apart, actually worked together, again, no drama! He drives our son to the graduation party. Before our son exists the vehicle, his father pulls him in for a tight embrace reminding him how much he's loved; an intentional fist bump capped off with an, "I'm proud of you son"! During the drive home, great conversation, lots of laughing and holding hands, our normal. At 12:15 PM we arrive home, my husband exits the vehicle; I walk around to the driver's side. Loving kisses, lingering embrace, and I love you exchanged.

Our daughter, who's in the back seat, sees us kissing and says "daddy, what about me"! He walks around to the rear passenger side where she is seated; he opens the door and plants a kiss on her lips and forehead. He says I love you, baby!

She responds, "I love you more daddy!" Before he walks off to head inside, I inquire about dinner later for the day. His response, "we can discuss it upon your return." More I love you exchanged. I watch him turn and walk into the garage, the door slowly lowers. I drive off to run more errands. Four o'clock PM, the children and I are close to home, and the music on the radio is blaring as we sing along to our favorite song. We pull into the garage, and everyone exits the vehicle and heads inside. A blood curling scream from my son; Dad is passed out on the floor of the gym, in the basement! I drop everything, screaming call 911! I descend the basement steps in record time, floating, never touching one. I touch him and instantly I knew he had transitioned to the other side. Hello, home free, at last, basking in the presence and staring into the face of our Lord!

Shock! Denial! Disbelief! All the air sucked out the room! Screaming, shouting, and crying! Praying, Lord NO! Please send him back! We need him! The Lord says, I'm NOT sending him back! Do you TRUST ME? Blur! Zombie, going thru the motions! Can't eat or sleep! Homegoing arrangements and song selections made. The obituary is written. Friday wake. Saturday home going celebration in Georgia. Monday laid to rest in Florida. Me standing over the casket of the man of my dreams, my very best friend on this side, my lover, boyfriend, confidant, cheerleader, encourager, sidekick, helpmate, comedian, and babies' daddy, taking his final rest. After what seemed to be an eternity, I bend over, kiss the casket, and I say, this is not goodbye, but hello when we finally see one another face to face again!

My husband was 48 years young when he was diagnosed with stage 4 colon cancer; a non-smoker, the picture of health, no symptoms, and most importantly no family history. He never abused his body, drugs, or alcohol. Per the American

Cancer Society, African Americans have the highest death rate and shortest survival of any racial and ethnic group in the United States for most cancers. I encourage every reader, especially African Americans to not wait until the age of 45 to be screened for colon cancer. You may not make it to 45 if you wait! Please get screened now if you've noticed blood in your stool, a change in your bowel habits, stool consistency, developed constipation, diarrhea, and excessive gas/bloating. I encourage every reader to get educated on colon cancer signs, symptoms, and facts by logging onto the American Cancer Society website at www.cancer.org

Finally, I implore you, the reader, if you are not saved to confess your sins, invite Jesus into your heart, and develop a personal, vertical relationship with God, by connecting with a Bible-based church. It is my testimony to each of you that God is the one and only true and living God. He is intentional and faithful in all His ways. He will never leave nor forsake those who diligently seek Him and are called by His name!

MY JOURNEY IN THIS THING CALLED LIFE
Nicole Moody-Sewell

It was the summer of 1985 when I first met this handsome young man with the heavy deep sexy voice saying to me "How you doing? I am John." I was like, DAG ON THAT VOICE! AND HE'S FINE TOO! Our relationship didn't happen right away. Luther Vandross was coming to town, so I thought maybe I'll say something to him about the concert. Well, I said to him, "Luther is coming to town would you like to go with me?" A couple of days later he came to me with the tickets. That was our first date and the beginning of John and Nicole.

John had a laid back chilled personality which was a good thing because I am the total opposite of that (smile). John adored and loved our children with everything in him and was an Awesome loving Dad & Husband. He was very quiet until he got to know you. Once he got to know you OH MY GOODNESS! He loved to crack jokes. John was what I call 'REAL" because although he was a good man, he didn't sugar coat anything. He kept it real all the time. He loved sports especially football. Our son played high school and college football and our daughter was a football trainer in high school. I really miss the four us watching football together and debating the games. Football season was an exciting fun time in our home. John also loved music. Earth Wind & Fire was one of his all-time favorite bands and their songs were always playing in our home.

John and I got married August 1, 1987, in Baltimore, Maryland at St. Edwards Roman Catholic Church. Our marriage wasn't perfect but it was perfect for us and I am grateful to God for the memories. We have a son, Javod, and a daughter, Sasha. The four of us relocated to Atlanta, Georgia in January of 1998. That was the best decision ever. The move made us even closer as a family because it was just the four of us; The Sewell Family.

July 26, 2015, my whole world flipped totally upside down when my husband, best friend, lover, & babies' dad closed his eyes right before me. He had a massive heart attack at the age of fifty years old. I knew my life as I knew it would never ever be the same. We buried John on August 1, 2015, which was our 28th wedding anniversary.

I thought why and how could this happen to us now, especially since our daughter, who is our youngest, had just graduated from college. Both of our kids had finished college, and we were so looking forward to our time. Adjusting to being alone, a "Widow" which was a word I just couldn't bring myself to say for a long time, was one of the hardest things I ever had to endure. I honestly didn't know how I was going to live without the man I had loved and had been with since I was twenty years old. I leaned deeply on my Faith and developed an even stronger relationship with God. Our son and daughter, whom I lovingly call our two heartbeats, also gave me the will to do my best to make it through each day.

When you are grieving the loss of your spouse, you will experience what I call a rollercoaster of emotions. The emotions you will experience range from depression to anger. I think it's important to attend grief counseling or join a bereavement support group to help you deal with the grieving process. I participated in a bereavement support group at a church because I needed a group that was Faith based. Talking with people who are experiencing or who have experienced the loss of a spouse is very helpful. Expressing your feelings and talking when you are ready helps you tremendously deal with the process of grieving. Never feel like you have to endure this grief alone because you don't. Your circle of family and friends will reach out to you. Let them help you. I was very Blessed to have my family, friends, and church family prayers, love, and support.

It's been three years since I lost my husband and I am now at a place where I need and want to find my happy again. Experiencing the loss of my beloved husband has really taught me just how precious life is and how important it is to live, love, and laugh. I know if John could speak to me from Heaven above, he would tell me "Nik, Baby you got this." He was always my biggest supporter.

I had gone out with a man that I used to talk to when I was a teenager however, we had been friends for many years. My first time going out with him was a little intimidating for me. I had been with the same man for over twenty-eight years, so that was very different for me to say the least. But he made me feel comfortable, and for that I am grateful. I remember feeling very nervous when we first kissed. That kiss started the fading away of the numbness I was feeling. Our friendship will not blossom into anything serious but, I am thankful for the experience because it allowed me to realize that am ready to begin my new journey of finding love again.

I'm ready for love again, but I am not trying to find what John and I had because that could never be duplicated. It's also important for me to be with a man who will not be intimidated by my late beloved husband because I will always celebrate his life. Time does help with healing. Just three years ago I couldn't imagine the thought of another man in my life. This doesn't mean you stop loving or missing your beloved spouse. It just means you are ready to move forward with life and loving again.

FOREVER LOVE
Bernard Shaw

"I know I have been sick for a while and haven't been the kind of wife you deserve. Are you going to leave me?" I looked my wife straight in the eyes and said, "Wherever I go, I'm taking you with me, either on my arm or in my arms. I will never leave you." With that said, we shared a warm embrace with tears welling in our eyes.

We knew that God had brought us together and that nothing would break us apart. Having met, working at the same office, the long conversations, shared laughter and mutual respect we had for each other, was realized in a matter of months. Our co-workers saw us as a strong couple before our deep friendship led to a romantic relationship. They regularly referred to her as my "Work wife" and me as her "Work Husband."

One night while we were dating, we sat next to each other on a leather reclining love seat, watching Netflix movies all night, talking, laughing and enjoying each other's company.

We had no idea we had stayed up that long until we saw the sunrise the next morning! This happened many times, even after we got married.

My wife, who had been beaten by a gang and left for dead as a teenager, who became an award-winning inspirational and motivational speaker, who landed a recurring speaking role on the television show NYPD Blue and after that, earned a Grammy Nomination, beat the odds many times throughout her life. She was afforded the opportunity to meet and establish business relationships with many well-known celebrities. At the height of her burgeoning acting career, she suffered a debilitating stroke that took her out of day-to-day interactions with others. She moved back home to recover and help care for her ailing mother who was suffering from COPD. As her mother was moving closer to having God call her back to heaven, the stress of knowing the end was near, weighed heavily on Sherri. She did all she could to comfort her and heal from the stroke.

After her mother's passing, Sherri moved to Virginia to be with her father who was an Air Force veteran. Her father was facing health issues himself, unbeknownst to Sherri, at the time. Her father stepped in after she was beaten by the gang and helped her regain the mental strength to forge ahead and not let life's challenges hold her back. Her parents had divorced a few years earlier, and the impact her father had on Sherri was immeasurable in helping her recover from the stroke, her mother's death and making it in the entertainment industry. People wondered how she was able to maintain so many relationships with celebrities, mainly male. She said she did not sleep with them and that was the main reason they respected her and maintained working relationships.

Shortly after our wedding day, my wife faced a life-threatening medical condition. There were many nights that she had cried in my arms from the pain she was enduring, asking me if she was going to live to see the next day. I always held her tight in my arms and told her, "Baby, you're the strongest lady I have ever known, and you will make it through this." After a six-hour surgery and the surgeon telling me that before the surgery, she only had days to live, I thanked God for answering our prayers. Sherri recovered, and after a few months, we both walked in the Atlanta 5K Peachtree Road Race. We finished the event with hands raised in triumph!

Sherri battled numerous chronic medical conditions while we were married and relied on her faith in God and my support to make it through. No one outside of our marriage had any idea of what she was dealing with. Her face never showed the pain she endured. Her pain management doctor commented that she was amazed that Sherri looked so beautiful while dealing with so many health conditions. Her skin was always so clear and smooth, embracing a vibrant smile and clear eyes. And yes, she had a beautiful, sexy body, with legs that were once insured for a million dollars!

We moved to Atlanta to allow her to pursue her acting career again. She had appeared in many movies including Lean on Me, Boomerang, Drumline, and Boycott (an HBO production). Her singing voice was also a great asset which led to her Grammy Nomination. She even opened for Jill Scott at a concert! The last movie, in which she appeared, Selma, allowed her the opportunity to sit down and talk to Oprah, one on one! She treasured that interaction and was honored that Oprah engaged her in the brief conversation centered on the passing of Maya Angelou, whom they both knew personally.

As her health was taking a turn for the worse, I always hugged, kissed and held her in my arms, praying that God would bring her through as He had done so many times before. I knew that God was going to call her back and I comforted her in every way possible. When that day came, I had no idea of the emotional pain I would endure from losing the love of my life. Not a day goes by that I do not think of her smile, her wit, and strength. When she passed, she knew she had experienced what many wives seek and only a few find: "Everlasting, unconditional love from her husband who will always be in love with her."

For others who have lost their loved ones, always remember that the memories of the good times will last forever. Thinking about a loved one who has passed is a celebration of the joy and happiness you shared. Although the pain of loss can be difficult to endure, the pleasure of fond memories will always help in the healing process.

FOREVER AND A DAY
Kimetha Spoon

April 2, 2016, will forever be engrained in my mind and my heart because that was the beginning of a life change that I did not see coming. We take so much for granted. Especially those of us who are strong women because we believe we are in control and have a handle on everything going on around us. I beg to differ since the angel of death knocked on my door and the one person who had been constant in my life for over 35 years was no longer there to be my rock, my confidant, my Boaz, my best friend, my lover and my protector.

Calvin and I met right after I graduated high school in 1979. I remember so vividly the phone calls he would make to me, letting me know that my future was with him and he was willing to wait forever. No matter how long it would take. He would sing "My Girl" to me over the phone, and of course, I was all smiles and felt giggly inside. The old saying that opposites attract is so true. Calvin and I come from totally different backgrounds. Our goals were different too. He was eight years older than me, had lived on his own, been in multiple relationships and had children. Mr. Spoon was adamant that he was going to create a life with me that only I dreamed about.

Our relationship wasn't a fairy tale because it came with issues, heartbreaks, trouble, and tears as well as days filled with joy, peace, happiness, and laughter smothered in a whole lot of love. Wow!! What a journey we had for the next 15 years. There were highs, but the lows taught me how to be a survivor. Calvin was instrumental in me learning to survive in the big world. I had never lived on my own nor had to fend for myself. He would say "Baby you have a lot of book knowledge but no street sense." Life was good until Calvin developed a drug problem that Satan intended to use to wipe him and us out!! But God said differently.

In 1996 God opened the door for us to change our scenery and move to Atlanta, GA where we knew no one. We had a fresh start in life. Calvin promised me that everything his addiction stole from us, he was going to replace. Our love was a forever and day type of love. We embraced the good with the bad. Over the next 20 years, God blessed us to live a comfortable life. Did we have challenges? Yes! Was it perfect? No! In spite of the losses we had encountered, we gained so much more. Calvin's love for me was that "for real" love many people dream of having. He may not have had the formal education, wore the three-piece suits, worked in corporate America or spoke politically correct, but he drew people to him because he was real and genuine.

In 2005, Calvin had been diagnosed with heart disease which required heart surgery placing six stents in his valves. We thought we had a lifetime together because he seemed too had beaten the odds associated with the heart disease. We had several scares over the years, but he always pulled through. He was released from the hospital on March 25, 2016, after one of those scares but we were assured he was ok to go home. Five days later we find ourselves back at the hospital but this time with a STROKE!! We thought that we would be ok because we had gotten to the hospital promptly and the TPA was administered. The doctor shared there was only a 2% chance of bleeding on the brain. My GOD who would have thought Calvin would have encountered that 2%. The image of him is grabbing his head from the pain and turning over to face me, and me not being able to understand a word he was saying is unthinkable. Being told that he was bleeding on the brain, he had to be sedated, and the process of looking for a hospital to transfer to for surgery was overwhelming. Before them sedating him, my son stood beside his bed and assured him, "Dad I got it!" while his dad was looking at me and me trying to be strong because I didn't want him to see the tears and fear. I regret not saying to him "I love you" "Fight" and "We will get through this together" "Remember Forever and a day." I had no idea that when he closed his eyes, they would never open again.

Death isn't something you prepare for daily. Making that decision to remove him from the ventilator was one of the hardest decisions that I have ever made in my life. I questioned God. Why? I questioned myself, wondering if I made the right decisions from the start of this life-changing event. I was angry, hurt, numb, terrified and yet I knew I had to be strong because that's what he would have wanted me to be.

The grieving process can be day to day and sometimes minute by minute. I believed in God and being an Elder in the church, I understood death, but it still did not mean I was immune to grief. I had to go through it, and I sought counseling. I looked great on the outside, but my inner man was crumbling. A song, a word or memory could bring tears to my eyes. What I have learned is not to hide it or try to escape from it, but go through it because it's natural. There are no set time limits for the process. But what I do know is that God has sustained me, and I am stronger two years later in coping with the death of my dear beloved husband. Our love existed, and it's nothing to hide from because it was and is Forever and a day!!!

A SECOND CHANCE AT LOVE
Deborah Warren

May 22, 2009, would mark the end of a love story that had been in the making since 1978.

Our story began in seventh grade at St. Anthony's/St. Joseph's Catholic School. When I first met Gary Rogers Warren, I didn't like him at all! I remember the first conversation we had, "he'd asked me if I had a boyfriend," and I told him yes, I did. He insisted on us getting to know each other. I told him "I don't think so!" As the school year progressed, I would not have much to say to Gary.

Once we started our eighth-grade year, I decided to be open to the possibility of Gary and I being friends. With my seventh-grade boyfriend being a year older than me, he was now in high school, and Gary made sure to take advantage of his absence. As the year went on, he knew that he had started to win me over and before I realized what happened "he had asked if I would be his girlfriend." "I said yes." This was the start of our love story!

Before entering high school, I expressed to Gary that I felt it would be better if we were just friends since we would be at different schools and it would probably be difficult to make a relationship work. Throughout our high school years, we dated other people, but we would keep in touch and even see each other occasionally. Especially during basketball season as he played for his high school team and I was a cheerleader for mine. Even on those occasions, I would melt when I saw him, but I wouldn't let him know that. The summer before entering college we would have plenty of conversations about life and how excited we were about college and being away from home.

During our college years, we continued our friendship, but I felt it had become something deeper. We had grown to become best friends and looked to each other for guidance as we embarked on adulthood. After two years of college, Gary decided to join the United States Air Force. I continued with college and graduated from Southern University. After graduation, I was engaged to be married to my college sweetheart. I was very excited about the new chapter I was about to start and wanted to share it with my best friend. I wanted to be sure that I had his blessings. Even though Gary gave me his blessings, for the next six years, I didn't have any communications with my best friend and first love.

In 1995, I separated from my husband. My daughter and I moved back to Pensacola, FL. During this time, I focused on adjusting to my new life and providing some stability for my daughter. In 1996, I would run into Gary's mom. She knew that I had moved back home through a mutual family friend. After a brief conversation, she would proceed to give me Gary's contact information and said "give him a call he would love to hear from you!" And that's exactly what I did. That's when we would be given "A Second Chance at Love"!

From that first conversation we had in 1996 after six years of no contact it felt as though we hadn't skipped a beat! After about six months of dating, Gary said to me "God has given me a second chance, and I'm not going to let you get away this time." He asked me to marry him, and of course, I said "yes"! On May 23, 1997, I would marry my best friend and soul mate!

Gary was a great father and husband. After we were married, Gary had to update his information to include us in the military system. He was not happy that they wanted to list De'Juener as his stepdaughter as he never looked at her in that way and wanted them to change it to show daughter. Because of policy, they couldn't change it. Even though I knew Gary loved my daughter, this process would show me just how much he cared about her. Even after the birth of our son Gary II, at no time did he ever treat her differently. While we were stationed at Bitburg/Spangdahlem Air Base Germany, we would welcome a bouncing baby boy (Gavin Isaiah) to our family; this was truly a surprise to us seeing as though we were under the assumption that I couldn't have any more kids. In 2004, we left Germany and headed stateside to Valdosta, GA.

Fast forward to 2009; the month of May should have been a time of celebration for the Warren Family. May 23, 2009, De'Juener was graduating from high school, and Gary and I were to celebrate our 12th year wedding anniversary. Instead May 22, 2009, the Warren Family was struck with grief and our lives would be forever changed as we lost a Loving Husband and Father at the age of 44.

My mom had come down that Thursday to help Gary and I prepare the house to receive family and friends for our daughter's graduation. Before going to bed that night I kissed Gary and said: "I Love You!" I had no idea this would be the last time I would get to say those words to him or feel his lips on mine. I was awakened by the faint sound of him calling my name. I was devastated when I walked into the bathroom to find him passed out on the floor. I immediately called out to my mother as I was in shock and also dialing 911. I had my mom keep the kids in their rooms because if this was going to be the last image of their father, I didn't want that to be it. I decided to send everyone to their prospective places as I went to the hospital to find out the fate of my husband. When the Chaplain of the hospital came through those doors, I became weak and knew that my love was gone! Not in a million years would I have thought those 24 hours before I would be calling family and friends and giving them the news of Gary's death. Everyone wanted to know was I still planning to celebrate De'. I told them yes because Gary would have wanted us to celebrate her accomplishments.

It took me going to therapy to help me realize that Gary's death wasn't my fault and I would have to continue living not only for myself but also for my kids. Gary and I tried to figure out why God had blessed us with this life after we had taken measures not to have any more kids. When the doctor said to us "this baby is here because of Divine Intervention" we paid attention. It came full circle on why Gavin Isaiah Warren was born. He was my Divine Intervention! God knew that I would need Gavin to get me through this problematic time in my life.

With this new life, I had to learn how to live life again without my "Soul Mate," the man that God had brought back to me after six years of no contact. The man I thought I would take late night walks with and experience life with until we were old and gray had diminished. Being widowed has been challenging in many aspects; having to raise young men,

—

dating, and learning how to become a handy woman around the house. YouTube and I are on a first name basis. LOL!

I would encourage anyone who may find themselves in this place to remember Philippians 4:13. I can do all things through Jesus Christ who strengthens me! You will still have your days but know that tomorrow is another day of life and another day of healing!

YOUR MAKER IS YOUR HUSBAND
THE LORD ALMIGHTY IS HIS NAME
Linda Webb

I met Rodney back in 2008 at our place of employment. We worked together for three years before noticing each other's charm. In March of 2011, I was on my way home from work when Rodney and I ran into each other walking down the walkway to our vehicles. He came to work in the evening at 3 pm as I was getting off work around that time. My workday started at 2 am. We all worked 12 to 14 hours a day driving tractor- trailers.

One day I received a notice from my doctor about my surgery date. I was getting off work that evening, myself along with some of the other drivers were standing at the fuel isle to fuel the truck. After a day's work, Rodney came through the gate and walked over to speak. I told him that I would be out for six weeks. He proceeded to give me his number and asked me to call him a week after my surgery.

Two weeks after my surgery, I gave him a call. He was stunned that I called him. Rodney invited me over to his place, and we immediately hit it off. Our feelings for each other began to grow. Six months later we realized that we were falling in love, so we decided to make it official by becoming boyfriend and girlfriend.

At the time, we were so deep into each other with our feelings that we decided to set a wedding date. We were enjoying each other, going on cruises together, and looking for places to live. We found a beautiful home in Stockbridge, GA. It was a four bedroom and three bath home. In August of 2012, two months after moving into our new home, we got married.

In addition to traveling together, and we worked the same shift together. We spent all of our time together. Vacations, work, everything we did, we did together. We hardly had any time off from each other the first three years of marriage. We concluded that we should work different hours!

By the fourth year of our marriage, although we worked different hours, we still had the same off days and vacation days together. By the fifth year of marriage, we had our upcoming vacation days planned out. Rodney decided to surprise me with something different. He took me to the Harley Davidson shop to purchase a motorcycle. We were supposed to ride out to Savannah on our 5th anniversary. Now I already have my endorsement for a motorcycle. My husband wanted to get his endorsement, but he decided to get the bike first before taking the course. So I asked the guy not to sell it to him, but my husband insisted that he get the bike first, and then get his endorsement. I said, "no that's backward," but he replied: "I am grown!" Since my husband was in the Marines, he was very hard-headed. I just threw my hands up.

Once the bike got delivered to the house, the delivery guy asked Rodney if he wanted to ride the bike to the garage. Rodney looked at me and told me to ride it. I said, "No let the delivery guy put it in the garage." So he did, and when the guy left, we just stood around looking at the bike before deciding to go into the house and eat our dinner. After dinner, we decided to go back outside because Rodney wanted to sit on the bike to see what it felt like. I told him to be careful and to be sure that the bike was in neutral. I was standing right next to him when all of sudden he hit the "on" switch. The bike crunk, and he starts struggling. I tried to grab the brakes, but the bike took off! Rodney was shocked as the bike hit the curve and threw him three stories high. I was screaming "No! Rodney! No! My God" My husband looked like a ragdoll falling from the sky. He hit an air condition unit as he came down and hit the ground. I was so scared! Tears were running down my face as I ran to see if he was still alive. I looked behind the shrubs where the unit was, and I saw his feet hanging from a small piece of skin from his legs. "Oh, my Goodness he was in a fetal position! Someone in the neighborhood came over and told me that he was still breathing, but I wasn't sure. I was in shock, screaming and hollering. I knew that I had lost my husband!

Once the cops arrived, they called a life flight helicopter to Grady Memorial Hospital. He was on life support for two weeks before he decided to go with our Lord Jesus Christ. Rodney passed on August 12, 2017, one week before our anniversary. Since his death, I have posttraumatic distress, and I am seeking Therapy. I hang out with my God sister Shenita Connally, and I Thank God for her.

As human beings, we are limited in what we can provide for those we love. Our resources, both material and emotional are finite, but God has no limits. He blesses His children far beyond our comprehension. He does more than just rain down His blessings on us. He sends abundant showers of blessing in every season of our lives. You are a rich woman and man once you see all God has provided for you.

LOVE CONQUERS
Cassandra Weems

It was a beautiful day on September 18, 2000. I left work early to get home so that I could spend time with my husband, Anthony, before going out to dinner for his birthday. When I arrived home, Anthony told me that he wanted to go and play racquetball before we went out to dinner. I said that was fine, but I was not comfortable with the idea because it had been some years since Anthony played racquetball. We used to compete with each other and other teams in racquetball in previous years when Anthony was active in the military. I prepared to go to the Department of Motor Vehicles (DMV) to renew the car license tag. We both left the house at the same time. Anthony headed to the racquetball club, and I was enroute to the DMV. We approached a red light when Anthony blew the horn to get my attention. I thought he was trying to tell me something was wrong with the car. When I rolled down the window, Anthony ran to the car and said: "I just wanted to tell you I love you."

I met Anthony Weems while we were in high school. I was going to the 10th grade, and he was going to the 11th grade, at different schools. Our first glance of each other happened at the Mall West End in Atlanta, Georgia. He was attractive, and his outgoing personality was evident. He had a smile that would brighten up a room. As we started our courtship, his attraction for me was displayed through his actions. Anthony would hold my hand. He wrote poetry and read it to me. We both loved dancing, and we didn't hesitate to dance when a tune we liked was playing. It did not take long for us to realize we had something special. He enjoyed telling jokes and bringing laughter to me and others around him. We spent a lot of time together throughout our high school years. Anthony joined the Army, and our love for each other flourished. Through this love, we created our beautiful daughter, Dysha. Anthony asked for my hand in marriage, and I accepted. We were married on November 20, 1981.

Well, getting back to September 18, 2000. I was excited about having dinner with my husband. I had left the DMV and still had time to fill while waiting for Anthony to finish playing racquetball. I decided to go check out a computer we were considering purchasing. The computer store was across the street from where Anthony was playing racquetball. When I arrived at the store, I noticed a fire truck and paramedic van at the racquetball facility. My spirit told me to go and see what was going on. As I proceeded to cross the street, my heart started pumping into overdrive. I went through the door of the facility... My body froze. Anthony was lying on the floor as the paramedics worked on him trying to get a pulse. I felt like I was having an out of body experience. Finally, the paramedics put him on a stretcher and transported him to the van. I climbed in the front seat of the van and just started praying. The ride to the hospital seemed like it took hours. I called my family and our pastor; they showed up at the hospital. We waited in the family room until the doctor came out of the emergency room, and said: "I'm sorry we did all we could, Anthony is gone." Surely, I was in shock and disbelief, even though I felt he was gone when we arrived at the hospital. The confirmation from the doctor made it reality. My immediate thoughts were....Anthony was physically fit, he had just seen the doctor for his yearly physical two weeks prior to this incident, and he just retired from the Army five years prior to this and we were just starting our second life. I thought we had a lot of years left together to love on each other. My mind was racing, thinking about a hundred and one things. First and foremost, how I was going to tell our daughter, who was away in her first year of college, that her Father was dead. After informing our daughter, and getting her back home, I needed some time to process what had transpired. Anthony and I had spoken about death and had our affairs in order, but the preparations were still heart wrenching to go through. I was operating in zombie mode. The days leading up to the celebration were a blur. My daughter and I made it through the funeral preparations and the home going celebration with the help of family and friends.

Now what? I gradually came to the realization that I was a widow at 38 years old, after being married for 18 years, and had lost the love of my life. Living life without my husband started to take its toll. All kind of emotions were beating me up – anger, loneliness, confusion, fear and the dreadful grief. The emotions I experienced were extremely difficult because of Anthony's sudden death of Coronary Artery Disease. There were no warning signs leading up to this episode. After getting my daughter back to college, my days were empty, and they seemed long. There were days when I didn't leave the house.

People would call to check on me, and I would tell them I couldn't talk because sometimes I just felt like waddling in my despair. Being a widow was looking pretty grim. The anger I felt towards God was real. I could not sleep, eat, or focus. Anthony and I had been inseparable; our love was enduring, so the loneliness felt was deep. Some days my crying was frequent, and the tears would flow. When the emotions would swell up inside of me, it didn't matter where I was I allowed nature to take its course.

My family and friends were around to console me during this time. They told me, "Anytime you need to talk just call, it doesn't matter what time it is." Of course, I took them up on their offer. Many nights, my mind was in chaos, and it was challenging for me to sleep. I used my lifeline and called someone to talk through what happened and express my feelings, and they would listen without giving feedback, which was crucial at this early stage of my grief. Sometimes all we need is a listening ear.

Depression began to creep up on me and I did not know how to handle it. Even though I was angry with God, I still cried out to Him for help. There was a grief support group that met at the hospital where Anthony was pronounced dead. My first thought was that I can't go back into that hospital. As a matter of fact, I did not even want to drive by the hospital. A voice spoke to me and said, "This is where you need to go to start processing the grief and regain control over your life." So, I composed myself and went to a meeting. My first visit turned out to be a listening session from others who loved ones were deceased. After attending several meetings, the facilitator asked if I was ready to share. It was the opportune moment for me to divulge my journey of becoming a widow and my feelings as a widow.

—

After that night, I felt a release in my spirit. The support group was good, and it allowed me to share with others who understood the cycle, but more was needed to help with the void I was feeling in my life from the absence of the love Anthony and I shared with one another. It was then that I decided to seek professional counseling by seeing a psychologist. Little did I know that the dialogue would be a one-way conversation with me doing all the talking. It was hard for me to speak freely to a stranger and share my feelings. This was new territory to me and out of my element. During one of the sessions with the psychologist, it was suggested that an appointment be made to see a psychiatrist to help with my insomnia and depression. An appointment was scheduled to see a psychiatrist. The visit with the psychiatrist was better in terms of dialogue; it was a little more comfortable since I had been through the clinical protocol with the psychologist. I left with a prescription to assist me with the insomnia and depression. After taking the medicine for a period, it seemed not to work for me, and I didn't want to become dependent upon it. So, I made the decision to stop popping the pills.

My process to get through the grief cycle continued, there were highs and lows that kept my emotions unstable. I was able to push through by attending the grief support meetings, going to church and being active in ministries, visiting with the doctors, interacting with family and friends and returning to work after being off for an extended period. It was not an easy journey, but I managed to prevail at a pace that worked for me.

The onset of becoming a widow put me in a desolate, frightening, and confused space. My decisions made during this transition made the difference in how I was able to make it through this valley of circumstances and try to have peace. The decisions helped me to understand there was nothing I could have done to keep my husband on this earth. I came to the realization that people couldn't tell me how to grieve or how long it would take to get through the grieving process. My mission was to work through it and not be concerned about how it looked or what others said. Finally, it felt like normalcy was returning to my life. The day came when a genuine smile returned. Talking about Anthony without crying ceased, laughter welled in my belly, being around others was pleasant, my life seemed in order. I felt like dancing again. It took me a while to get over my anger with God, but when I did, God's love was revealed to me in my husband's transition. The revelation was that God gave my husband life and his angel wings on the same day - September 18. This revelation helped me get through my grief.

The adage "be careful what you say to people because it might be your last words" rang true on September 18, 2000. The last words we spoke to one another were "I Love You." I am thankful that Anthony and I expressed our love for one another throughout our marriage, but particularly on that day, and my conscious is clear. It's hard enough to deal with the grief without incorporating regrets.

To you the reader, always live life to its fullest and incorporate laughter. My husband transitioned at the young age of 39, we thought we still had time to create a lot more memories. Don't let the chaos of this world hinder your relationship with the ones you love. Make time to create lasting memories with family and friends. Trust and believe that you can do all things through Christ who strengthens you (Philippians 4:13).

What I learned through the grief process, and being a widow is that love conquers all and it is rooted within our heart, spirit, and mind. It does not have to be tangible to be felt. I feel that love from our heavenly Father every day, as well as from the love Anthony and I shared for many years.

UNTIL DEATH DO US PART
Shenita Connally

My love for Winston Connally will always abide in my heart regardless of where life's journey takes me!!

It all started back in the summer of 2003. Youth Under Construction, Inc. launched its first summer camp. This was a God-given PURPOSE for me after losing my mother unexpectedly in 2001. Winston's previous wife Elaine Connally invited me to sit around the table as an inaugural member in establishing the Clayton County Adolescent Coalition. We often met with other agencies to discuss strategies to bring more youth-serving organizations together for the greater good of our community.

Throughout the years I worked professionally close with Winston and Elaine before her passing in September 2009. We became extended family in the community. I never visited the Connally's home & neither did they visit mine, but we supported each other's efforts. We respected each other in such a way that if I needed a cook for one of my fundraisers, I would call Elaine and ask her if Winston was available to assist and without fail he would oblige. I was forever GRATEFUL for their support.

That relationship led me to a solid friendship with the man who later became the LOVE of my LIFE, after being single for 20 plus years until we married October 28, 2011 was truly a blessing. Our friendship was EXTRA SPECIAL because Winston shared his heart from day one about every aspect of his life; the good, bad, ugly and indifferent. He was so transparent that he told me he didn't like me during our working professional years because as he said "I thought you thought you were better than others but I was so wrong!" That was the beginning of our LOVE affair. I never looked at Winston in an attractive manner while he was married to Elaine, and later I realized I wasn't supposed to. It wasn't a part of the bigger plan for me.

As a result of our friendship, I was able to assist him during the grieving process. Eventually after a short period of time, he told me "you're a KEEPER!" No man had ever said that to me, and I knew he was the one. I was so glad I opened my heart to allow love in. Two years later, our friendship led to a Godly marriage. Elaine prepared Winston for the next phase of his life by telling him a few days before she transitioned that she wanted him to marry again. I would often tell him during our courtship that I needed to talk to Elaine about him and one night she appeared to me while I was driving their van, in my dream. She got in the van on the front passenger side smiling. I said to her "you finally came." After that dream, I knew without a shadow of a doubt that he was the one I would marry.

The courting phase was amazing. It included working together in the community, church, and our personal lives. If you saw one of us, more than likely you saw the other (Teheeheeee). That phase of our lives was so naturally magical in that it seemed like a dream come true to me after 20 years of being a single mom and now to have a PARTNER that you vibe so well with was amazing! Even the challenges on our journey seemed manageable. We both loved the Lord and wanted to please Him. Winston was ordained as a minister two months before we married and he took his calling very seriously. I was PROUD to walk alongside him as his LIFE partner for the rest of our lives together. I learned to love and respect him and he loved me to the core. He was not afraid to tell the world about the love he had for me.

On June 30, 2015, that dream became a nightmare around 10:30 pm when Winston laid down next to me to say our normal "I love you...Goodnight" sealed with a kiss. He collapsed right in front of my very own eyes. You see, we had a scare with his health six months after we married which resulted in heart and kidney failure. I fought for his life medically while he was down and my "Big Diddy" recovered by God's GRACE and MERCY (Winston's favorite saying). This time I thought would be no different in that he would certainly live to share yet another testimony about God's goodness. However, that was not the case. After twenty-one days of aggressive care along with fasting, praying, trusting and believing that he would recover, he did not. My life as I knew it was no longer, but the love for my husband continues to grow and abide in my heart today.

Team Connally's LOVE blessed so many people and gave hope to some who had given up on love. I'm so GRATEFUL to God that he saw fit to bless me with a man after His own heart, to love me as He instructed. Winston taught me so much in the almost six years we were blessed to journey together. An important part of the lesson that resonates with me today is "AGAPE Love." He demonstrated it daily and I learned to do the same during our walk together, even until this present day.

I pray that my story blessed you as you read it and the AGAPE Love we shared grabbed you and will be a part of your life-journey. Please live, love and laugh every chance you get! If you're not connected with your life partner, don't give up. If I kept the faith for 20 years until we discovered each other as friends, then lovers and 22 years until my second marriage, you can do the same.

My love for "Big Diddy" will always abide in my heart, but I have enough room to allow someone else to love me and for me to love them in return.

The ultimate lesson learned in my marriage to Winston Connally was...

"Marriage Takes Three"

Marriage takes three
to be complete;
It's not enough
for two to meet.
They must be
united in
By love's Creator,
God above.

Then their love will be
firm and strong:
Able to last when
things go wrong.
Because they've felt
God's love and know
He's always there,
He'll never go.

And they have both loved
Him in kind
With all their heart
and soul and mind;
And in that love
they've found the way
To love each other
every day.

A marriage that follows
God's plan
Takes more than
a woman and a man.
It needs a oneness
that can be
Only from Christ
"Marriage Takes Three!"

Author Unknown

"My Good Thang!"

I am just getting a chance to sit down and write this special note.

I would like to say Happy Birthday (October 16) to an amazing woman, the Love of my life my own Diva (Shenita). When I awaken each and every morning I thank the Lord for placing you in my life. I would like to take this time to thank you for being my confidante, my earthly rock (support), my best friend, the love of my life and a major part of Team Connally. The word says when a man finds a wife he finds a good thing, so hello my "good thang". I thank God, my love for you grows' stronger day by day and I pray that the Lord continues to allow me to love you like Christ loved the church. May the Good Lord continue to rain down blessings of love on you and grant you providence and peace.

Love Always,

Winston Connally
October 17, 2013

A MESSAGE FROM THE AUTHORS

We may never know the exact reason that motivated you to purchase this book, but we do know nothing happens accidentally, because our God is intentional about everything! We hope our Abiding Love stories are a testament to these truths. God is faithful and true love never dies! It is our sincere prayer that these stories resonate in your hearts and minds, restoring trust and faith in God when your spouse or loved one departs this earthly home.

We encourage you to live each day as if it is your last. Choosing to seize every opportunity to love without limits, laugh until it hurts, stress less, recognize beauty in simplicity, and carve out time to be purposefully present with your loved ones every day.

May you find and experience abiding love!

Meet The Authors

Janice Gregg Billingslea

Janice Gregg Billingslea is the widow of the late Burrell C. Billingslea II who made his heavenly transition four years ago on July 24, 2014. She is the mother of five wonderful children and six grandchildren. Janice is affectionately called "Mimi" by her grands. Janice says that her family is the "Wind beneath her wings." Janice has taken the untimely tragedy and trauma of the death of her beloved "Burrell" and used it as a catalyst to ignite all of the passion and fire within her to Live Life to its fullest, embracing each new day with God's Word and taking each step purposefully and intentionally.

Being a widow changed the trajectory of her life and with it came a total paradigm shift in the way that she lives her life and the way that she is now perceived by herself, family, friends, colleagues and community. Janice has used this experience as a voice to educate people on what she calls "widow etiquette."

Something that she feels the church has failed to do in the

Christian community. Part of this passion and fire is being harnessed at her church by her involvement in the Widows /Widowers Ministry at the Fellowship of Faith Church, International where she and Burrell attended as a family for over twenty-five years. Janice has utilized her talents and skills in coordinating activities that have taken the ministry outside the box.

She is following the path that she believes that God has paved for her. This journey has included three phases that she has walked through, Wilderness, Wandering and Worshipping. The first and second phases of Wilderness and Wondering included her seeking God and his direction in this new chapter of her life. The third phase Worshipping has brought new clarity and joy in the Lord and she is learning how to become content with God as the center of her life.

Janice's professional career includes over 25 years in Social Work working with children and families leading them from dependency to self-sufficiency and from homelessness to permanent housing. She has worked in both the private and non-profit sectors. She holds an Associate Degree in Behavioral Health from Atlanta Metropolitan College a B.S. Degree in Organizational Leadership from Mercer University.

Janice is also an entrepreneur. Trained as a life skills and job readiness facilitator, she is the founder and developer of a Life skills and Job Readiness Program called, "Bridge to Unspoken Destiny." Janice's passion is helping young women find their purpose, passion, and worth. She delivers life changing and effective self-esteem classes by utilizing individual comprehensive motivational curricula that she develops. Her training contracts have been with Work Force giants in the industry such as the City of Atlanta's Workforce Development Office, Atlanta Urban League, Grant Associates, and the City of Atlanta Housing Authority. Janice's latest achievement, which she is most proud of, is being the President of Discreetly Designed Medical Accessories, a medical garment company that was birthed out of her husband's long-term illness with congestive heart failure. The garments are designed for patients who carry life sustaining equipment such as left ventricular assist devices. The garment is called the InvisiVAD/LVAD T-shirt.

She enjoys monthly gatherings with her children, Jhmeid, Burrell, James and Joel and daughter Kali and grandchildren, Jhalen, Jhasmine, Anjhel, Jordon, Preston and Logon where they just enjoy each other catch up with family business. Janice hopes to remarry someday because she now knows the value of a good marriage and understands why it's so important, not to sweat the small stuff. Janice longs to experience Love on a greater level. Her husband, Burrell, pronounced a blessing on before he transitioned. She now lives by his words to her, "Your faithfulness has only been surpassed by God Himself, Go Live Your Life." Janice feels that this affirmation sustains her on this journey and God directs every footstep that she takes.

Rosalind Bishop

Rosalind Bishop is currently a Clinical Chaplain with Piedmont Healthcare System in Atlanta, Georgia. She holds a Doctorate of Healthcare Administration, Masters in Human Services/Nonprofit Management, Bachelor of Science in Business & Marketing, A Retail Marketing degree and multiple Clinical Pastoral Education certifications.

Ms. Bishop has over twenty years of entrepreneurial experience which hails a retail clothing store, beauty supply store & spa, multimedia entertainment company serving the music and entertainment industry for over fifteen years and her most recent establishment, a self-care retreat and healing center. Yet, with all of that, Ms. Bishop takes great pride in raising her five amazing children David (23), Daniel (21), Darius (17), Alaynah (10), Amaya (6). In spite of their loss they still continue to thrive. Her eldest child David, graduated from Morehouse College this year. Her children continue to be Ms. Bishop's motivation and inspiration.

Ms. Bishop is also author of 'Whispers of A Widow' written from her journey as a wife of eighteen years turned widow in ten minutes. You'll have to read the book!

The amount of wisdom, experience and compassion Rosalind has overflows into her passion for people and her health & life coaching career. Ms. Bishop's impact in the lives of many is immeasurable.

Johnny Causey

Johnny N. Causey "JC" was born in Pensacola, Florida, and is the fifth child of Mary Causey. JC he accepted the Lord as a young child but came into the true knowledge of Christ at age 14. He accepted his call into the ministry in November 1993, and was ordained in 1994 at Rock of Ages Holiness Church, under the Leadership of Bishop Ross O. Knight, Sr. Minister Causey was ordained as an Elder in 2002, while serving in Bahrain, as the Pastor of the Gospel Service in the Chapel. For the past 5 years, he has been the Assistant Pastor of the Miracle Christian Fellowship Center COGIC, Buffalo, NY.

Pastor JC was married to the late Aquilla Causey, who now rests with her Savior. They have four daughters Melissa, Sequoia, Ja'Neshia, and Courtney. He has a son-in-law, 2 grandchildren Naomi, and Da'Quan. Pastor JC is a sinner saved by grace, as well as an upcoming author.

Pastor JC received his education in Escambia County, and is a graduate of Booker T. Washington High School. He holds an Associates in Criminal Justice, Bachelors in Computer Programming, Bachelor in Church Ministry, Bachelor of Science in Criminology with a concentration in Sociology, he then furthered his education to pursue a Master's Degree at Trinity Evangelical Divinity School, Deerfield, IL studying Christian Studies and received a certificate towards his Master's Degree.

Franda Clay

Franda A. Clay is a native of Atlanta, Georgia. She resides there with her beautiful young adult daughters. Throughout her life, she endured the loss of her mother at age nine and the unexpected loss her husband at the age of 31, resulting in serious bouts of depression and anxiety. Both of these experiences pressed her to begin writing about her feelings as a way to cope with the losses. She says that, "It [writing] is my outlet. When I put pen to paper, I can see my path more clearly. It's like a roadmap to the future".

Her foundational Bible scripture is, none other than, Habakkuk 2:2-3, *"Then the Lord answered me and said, "Write the vision and engrave it plainly on [clay] tablets, so that the one who reads it will run. For the vision is yet for the appointed [future] time. It hurries toward the goal [of fulfillment]; it will not fail. Even though it delays, wait [patiently] for it, because it will certainly not delay."*

She is also passionate about helping and inspiring others through her personal experiences. As she states, "I believe God allows me to go through certain experiences in life so that I can create a story or give it a voice". When she is not writing, she uses her Master's degree to teach accounting and management courses at a local community college in Atlanta. In a few short months, she will become Dr. Franda A. Clay. Her hobbies include CrossFit and a number of other outdoor activities.

She is the self-published author of "The Husband Journal". The book was inspired by some of her failed previous relationships. The book description reads, [Join one woman's journey through pain, healing, and purpose to God's ordained husband. After years of trying to get it right, the author realized that her destined time to meet her future husband is in the hands of God. Travel with her as she recalls the events leading to the break-up of her last relationship that consisted of verbal and mental abuse, defiance against God's Word, and total emotional devastation. Her unique, spiritual encounter beyond comprehension is what finally opened her eyes and stopped the abusive relationship. She has found peace and assurance of God's promise by communicating with her future husband daily thorough her "Husband Journal"].

Sonia Lynn Davis

Sonia Lynn Davis is a servant leader who has been blessed to hold the titles of wife, mother, daughter, grandmother, aunt, sister, friend and more. She has a passion for helping others – embracing the philosophy that it's important to lift as you climb.

Professionally she serves as the Coordinator of Homeless Education for Clayton County Public Schools in Georgia where she ensures that homeless students are identified and served in compliance with the federal law. During her more than 20 years with Clayton County Public School, she has received both state and local recognition for excellence in providing support for the county's homeless population. Sonia's diligent efforts to create, sustain and expand one of the most successful Homeless Education programs in Georgia makes her a sought out speaker and mentor for those running similar programs in the southeast.

Prior to joining Clayton County Public Schools, Sonia headed the personnel training areas for Dobbs Houses, Inc. and also served as an independent consultant to provide strategic management support during the Host Marriott Corporation and Concessions Paschals takeover at Atlanta's Hartsfield International Airport. Before entering a corporate setting, she worked as a reading teacher for the MLK Center for Social Change and academic assistant to Dr. Christine King Farris.

Sonia serves as a member of the Board of Directors for Calvary Refugee Center and a charter member of Orange Duffel Bag Initiative Education Committee. She also is an active member of her church, New Testament Gospel Worldwide Ministries, where she serves as a member of its Executive Management Team.

She is a cum laude graduate from Spelman College, where she earned a bachelor's degree in Education, with a concentration in Child Development. She also holds a master's degree in Educational Management from Strayer University.

A native of Utica, New York, she currently resides in Stockbridge, GA. She is the proud mother of her adult daughter, Amanda, who is the apple of her and her late husband Jake's eye. She's also the grandmother of Faith whose name reflects the family's faith-focused life style.

In her spare time, she enjoys shopping, dining out and creating designs for her customer bracelet line, Embracelets by Sonia – charming the world one Embracelet at a time.

Keith Horton

Keith has over 31 years of leadership experience in both the military and state government. Keith spent over 20 years on active duty (Army) and held various leadership positions throughout the world before retiring from his last duty station, The Pentagon, at the rank of Lieutenant Colonel in 2006.

Immediately following retirement, he was hired as the Deputy Director of Georgia's Division of Child Support Services and a year later was appointed as the Director of Child Support Services. He served as the Child Support Services Director for five years, and in this capacity, he led the transformation of one of the lowest performing child support agencies to one of the best performing in the nation. In 2012, Keith led the transition of all vocational programs from the Department of Labor to the newly formed Georgia Vocational Rehabilitation Agency and later served as Deputy Director for the agency.

In July 2013, Governor Deal appointed Keith as the

Commissioner for the Georgia Department of Human Services (DHS). In this role, he was responsible for a $1.5 billion agency and over 8,000 employees that oversaw the provision of human services throughout Georgia. In July 2015, Keith transitioned from the Department of Human Services to his new role as Assistant Commissioner of the Department of Juvenile Justice.

Keith earned his Bachelor's Degree in Business Administration from Albany State College, a Master's of Science Degree from South Carolina State University and a Doctorate in Education from Argosy University.

Keith is a graduate of Clayton Leadership and Leadership Atlanta and a life member of Kappa Alpha Psi. He is a member of Cornerstone Fellowship Church in Fairburn Georgia and serves as Associate Pastor. Keith was blessed with a wife of 28 years before she recently passed away. They have two adult children who are both married and three grandchildren from their unions.

Veronica Lewis

Veronica Lewis, along with her late husband, Rudolph, is the co-founder of The Thelma Lewis Foundation/GrandMa's Hands. It is a local and privately funded program dedicated to assisting grandparents and others who are raising children that are not their own.

Born and bred in the south, she married her childhood sweetheart, Steven when she was 21. Together they bore two sons, Steven, II, and Toby. She was first widowed when she was only 31 years old. That time of her life left her broken, not only financially but mentally as well. Counseling as we know it today was not readily available, and so she was left feeling lost and all alone.

When she met her second husband, Rudolph, it was at a much-needed time in her life. For her, the sun began to shine again in her lives and the boys! A very short time after
meeting, they had one son together. They named him Chanz, both joking that he was her "last chance for a girl."

They found true happiness for themselves and the children. After 32 years, the unthinkable happened.... again. She was widowed in 2016, this time at the age of 63. Finding herself consumed in a different and very overwhelming grief, she took to pen and paper as she had in her youth. She began to share her story with many people on social media. In this uncommon way, God has allowed her to work through her grief by helping and ministering to others.

Because of the profound love and loss with these two marvelous men, she truly has a keen sense of what Abiding Love means.

Ebony Lewis-Hodge

EBONY LEWIS-HODGE is a native of Atlanta, GA, a woman of faith, and a mother of three, which includes a set of Storm Troopers – young fraternal twins she collectively refers to as "E2." Now a widow, she was married for five years to Jamal Hodge, had a blended family of six children, and a white dog, which is now pink and purple.

A graduate of Georgia State University, Ebony studied abroad in England, France, Italy and South Africa, and speaks basic Spanish, French, and Italian. Since childhood, she has enjoyed writing, which includes school newspapers, writing competitions, playwriting, and screenwriting. Throughout her adult life she has experimented with various occupations: photography, i.e., drugstore photo lab technician; acting, or more like "an Extra;" and corporate recruiting, which means recruiting to find her next corporate job.

Due to the tragic loss of her late husband Jamal, she used her pain to propel her purpose. As a licensed insurance professional preparing for her investment license, she is passionate about educating and helping families build financial wealth and preparing for the unexpected. For more information, you can follow her on:

• Instagram @ebonylewishodge
• Facebook.com/EbonyLewisHodge
• **www.ebonylewishodge.com**

Daina Matheny Logan

Daina Matheny Logan is a Practical Nurse and a newly Ordained Evangelist. To my union with Jamez Logan, we have one daughter and four grandsons. Two of the grandbabies are twins born a few days after my 50th birthday. What a wonderful gift. I am so grateful to have had 25 years with a man that I know God built just for me. Jamez never met a stranger and was my chocolate butter pecan covered angel with sprinkles on top. I thank God for a second chance at life. I'm young, not dumb but full of "hey watch yo self-goodness inside and out" I feel amazing in my own skin. God, Jesus and the Holy Spirit are my best friends, and I will never do anything without them. God said my latter shall be greater and I receive it and am walking in my overflow after the storm. My favorite song now is by Jason Nelson "Forever is a long time, that's how much I love you." Said the Lord.

Patricia Rivas

Patricia Cole Rivas is like a tree with deep roots, planted by a stream of living water. Though, firmly rooted and grounded in the Lord, she was tested and shaken to the core on May 30, 2015, with the sudden and unexpected transitioning of her beloved husband, the late Elder Chad Rivas, Sr.

Shaken, but not broken, Patricia's vertical relationship with the Lord went to new heights as she chose to praise, press, and push her way out of thoughts of murder-suicide and depression. She overcame by calling on the name of Jesus, trusting and believing in the one and only true and living God to keep her mind and her children. Not one to disappoint, God showed Himself faithful, allowing Patricia to see and experience miracles, signs and wonders of His love; taking Patricia to new and higher levels in Him thru praise and worship.

Patricia is not a professionally trained author or speaker, but has used the valleys of life as her training ground to propel her into her destiny; sharing the undeniable power and strength in the name of Jesus and encouraging listeners and readers of all ages to be proactive in learning more about screening for the risk of colon cancer, before age 45.

Patricia is the proud mother of two amazing and wonderful children who are perfect reminders of God's love, from her blessed union with Chad Rivas, Sr.

Nicole Moody-Sewell

Nicole Moody Sewell was born in Baltimore, Maryland on October 1, 1966. She graduated from Northern High School in 1984 and married John Francis Sewell, Jr in 1987.

She moved to Atlanta, Georgia in 1998 where she raised her son and daughter and was a full-time stay at home wife and mother. She was a Faithful member of Our Lady of Lourdes Catholic Church in Atlanta, Georgia and will forever call Lourdes her "Home Church."

Nicole now lives in Baltimore, Maryland where she is finding Happy again and living her journey called life after living in Atlanta for twenty years. She enjoys spending time with her family and is so very Blessed to be able to spend precious time with her Mother Mrs. Nannie Moody who is 78 years young, hanging out with her friends, enjoying her coffee at coffee shops like Starbucks & Chocolate' Coffee Shop, and eating Maryland steam crabs.

Bernard Shaw

As the third child, out of four born into a career military family, I understand the importance of being flexible, understanding and adaptable to any situation. Born in Wilmington, NC and having lived for several years in Europe, I have a positive outlook on the world in which we live. Although I enjoy reading, long walks and stimulating conversation, I am an extrovert to most and enjoy meeting new people. Life is what you make of it and I have lived by this credo for many years.

As a graduate of Norfolk State University, with a Bachelor of Science Degree in Biology, I entered corporate America working for over 10-years at Xerox Corporation as a Senior Marketing Executive. I achieved my goal there and earned their President's Club Award for performing in the top 10% of my peers nationally. Thereafter, I entered the medical device industry as a Spine Specialist with Acromed (bought out by Medtronics) and was their first African American in the country hired in that position. I have started several businesses in various industries over the years and currently work for a private, non-profit helping disabled veterans find employment.

My future offers one thing that most of us should heed and that is the opportunity to live life to the fullest! I have been blessed with excellent health all my life and will maintain a healthy, active lifestyle. I do not let little things get to me or worry about things that are out of my control. As the former NFL head coach Herman Edwards once said, "If you have a goal and do not have a plan to achieve that goal, then all you have is a wish!" My goal is to love like there is no tomorrow, seek happiness in whatever circumstances I encounter and treasure every minute I am given to make a positive impact on the lives of others! That is my plan and I'm sticking to it!

Kimetha Spoon

Kimetha Spoon is a strong independent woman who finds strength and courage to do all things through Christ. She has a love for people and believes there is good in everyone. Kimetha's life journey has taught her many valuable lessons over the years including how to mature into a loving, caring mother while still a teenager, defeat the odds of being on public assistance in spite of being one of eleven children, obtaining her Bachelors and Master degrees and how to move forward as a widow after 35 years of marriage. She is blessed beyond measure with two children - daughter Emily Thompson and son Calvin J. Spoon. She is fondly known as Nana to her five heartbeats – Kiara, Erick, KeJuan, Merka, and Merkell.

Kimetha loves being a blessing to others without expecting anything in return and loves her immediate, extended and church families unconditionally. She was ordained as an Elder in 2015 at Cornerstone Fellowship Church where she continues to work in the Education, Women and Youth Ministries.

Kimetha is co-owner of Love & Integrity Funeral Home Services in Greenville, TX along with her daughter Emily and business partner Detria Hill. History was made in March 2017 with the establishment of the funeral home being the first African American women opening and owning a funeral home in Hunt County. Our mission is to treat every family like our own - committed to offering families a meaningful life celebration for their loved ones.

Kimetha shares that her husband was her best friend and believed in her when she didn't. His death taught her many lessons, and her hopes are that through this journey she can share with others the importance of loving forever and a day.

Deborah Warren

Deborah Warren was born in the Sunshine State (Pensacola, FL) and is a believer in all people. She received a BS Degree in Business Education from Southern University and A&M College, Baton Rouge, Louisiana. After completing her degree, she taught school for over 11 years. As an educator, she has a spirit of instructing and equipping individuals with the knowledge they need to enhance their capabilities.

She has taught at many levels: elementary, secondary and post-secondary. She feels that education is the key to a successful life because it equips you with the knowledge of the world around you, the ability to be your best and have greater possibilities of a career path! Even after she moved on to the Federal Government, she continued her love of educating at the Child Development Center on the Air Force Military Bases. After leaving the world of education Deborah is now working as a Financial Specialist/Business Analyst for The US Fish and Wildlife, Department of The Interior and even in this position she has not stop educating as she finds herself instructing individuals on proper protocol and procedures.

Her life experiences have gotten her to this point of being a co-author of "Abiding Love!" Deborah lost her soul mate of 12 years becoming a widow on May 22, 2009, after her husband died of a heart attack. She is a mother of one daughter (De'Juener Rideau), two sons (Gary Warren II and Gavin Warren) and the proud GiGi of one grandson (Donovan Mathis) who has her twisted around his little finger.

Linda Webb

Linda Webb is a woman of faith. She is a mother of two and a grandmother of 3. Her son lives in Nashville, TN with his family. She lost her daughter at the age of 17 and is now raising her beautiful granddaughter whom she calls her angel. Most recently, Linda lost her husband in a fatal motorcycle accident in which she witnessed. Due to these unfortunate and untimely circumstances, Linda is now starting her new life as a widow and single mom. She is able to maintain and move forward through her faith and by the grace of God.

Linda has been a truck driver for 27 years and is now attending John Casablanca to start a new and exciting career in Model and Talent Management. Using writing as a form of therapy, Linda is a co-author of the new book, Abiding Love, where she shares the details of her love story with her late husband.

Cassandra Weems

Cassandra is a woman who truly believes all things are possible as long as faith is prevalent. The source of her contribution towards *"Abiding Love"* is her desire to help others. Cassandra feels that life is about sharing experiences that will enable others to realize that they do not have to face challenges alone and that a support system is never far away.

Spending time with family and friends is an important aspect of her life. Cassandra enjoys participating in fitness activities, traveling, experiencing new adventures and meeting new acquaintances. Volunteering in the community with varied organizations allows Cassandra to provide outreach in different capacities. She specializes in sharing smiles that she prays will uplift a person's spirit and make their day brighter.
After becoming a widow, Cassandra's determination to live included completing her Bachelor's degree while working full time as a Compliance Specialist for the U.S Department of Education; being an active mother to her delightful daughter;

and accepting the love of a wonderful man that God placed in her life. Cassandra realized her living could not stop with the death of her husband.

The message that she wants to impart to readers is that the *Abiding Love* for our dearly departed lies within and will always be a part of our lives.

Shenita Connally

Shenita Connally is a believer in new beginnings. As a mother, grandmother (affectionately called Nana) and widow, Shenita has seen her share of challenges. However, through her strong faith, relentless tenacity and deep desire to see people grow, Shenita is now committed to educating others on how to overcome obstacles and pursue a vibrant and blessed life.

As a certified life coach, college graduate and educator for the State of Georgia Public School System in Clayton County and the University of Georgia Cooperative Extension. Education is at the heart of what Shenita embraces. She uses her gifts of educating, encouraging and exhorting to help others strive for a better life through unique experiences, such as widowhood or parenting grandchildren at any the age.

Life with Shenita, LLC encompasses three initiatives that capture the passion and purpose of Shenita. Life After the

Rain is a program committed to helping others experience life again and recover from heartbreak and tragedy, specifically widows and widowers. The second initiative is educational with Is Your House in Order? - an initiative committed to helping people understand the importance of being financially fit and prepared for the inevitable. Her final initiative is called HYDRATE – a program encouraging the power and importance of staying hydrated, both physically and spiritually. As a woman embracing her new health and weight loss, she educates and encourages the necessity for water and faith to remain strong physically.

At the core of every initiative of Life with Shenita is the passion to see people overcome every obstacle and experience Life after the Rain.

She is a widow (husband died on July 21, 2015 as a, result of a heart attack o. June 30) with 3 biological children Raven A. Scott 35, Alvin J. Scott 31 and Brittnee Nicole Scott 29. To her union she gained 2 bonus sons, Christopher Winston Connally 31 and Jonathan W. Connally 27. Her grandchildren Micah Isaiah Morgan 13, Madison Treniece Scott 7, Wesley Alexander Tucker 4 & Genesis Alexandria Campbell 1 year old. Her grandchildren give LIFE a new meaning!

"Successful Marriages are Built on True and Genuine Friendship: Your spouse should be your Best Friend Forever. True friends spend time together; they talk together, laugh together and cry together. True friends enjoy each other's company while they celebrate life's moments together. True love is more than just kissing, hugging or sleeping together; it's about loyalty, honesty and courtesy - attributes that you'll always find in a best friend. Don't just love each other, take your marriage to the next level and become true best friends also; you'll have fun and enjoy life together. Genuine friendship creates wonderful marriages. Don't Just be your spouse's spouse; become your spouse's Best Friend Forever!"

- Isaac Kubvoruno

Made in the USA
Columbia, SC
13 February 2019